HOW SPEAKERS
MAKE PEOPLE LAUGH

HOW SPEAKERS MAKE PEOPLE LAUGH

Bob Bassindale

Parker Publishing Company, Inc.
West Nyack, New York

Two jokes from *10,000 Jokes, Toasts & Stories* by Lewis & Faye
Copeland. Copyright 1939, 1940 by Lewis and Faye Copeland. Copyright
© 1965 by Doubleday & Company, Inc. Reprinted by permission of
the publisher.

Library of Congress Cataloging in Publication Data

Bassindale, Bob,
   How speakers make people laugh.

   Includes index.
   1. Wit and humor--History and criticism. 2. Wit
and humor--Psychology. 3. Public speaking. I. Title.
PN6149.P5B35   808.7   76-14881
ISBN 0-13-434118-X

Printed in the United States of America

DEDICATION

To Jim Byron of Ft. Worth, my favorite
Texan, my favorite newsman, who, as much
as anyone I know, understands the real sense
of humor.

How This Book Will Help You

Whether you're a podium professional or a rostrum rookie, if laughter and humor are a puzzle to you, this book will help you find the missing pieces. It's a book on humor technique that really works!

If you've ever had problems telling a joke, finding the right humor for the right audience, editing or rewriting a gag to make it fit your style, your subject, or your argument, this book cannot fail to help you. If the idea of actually creating original humor seems as difficult as trying to do your own dental work, this book will not only help you, it will surprise you. It will prove that any intelligent person can learn the knack of creating original humor.

The fact is, humor is a mystery only to those who have never taken the trouble to explore it and learn its known principles and techniques. Humor does not suffer from a lack of knowledge. It suffers from neglect. If business and professional men and women would spend as much effort studying, practicing, and perfecting humor technique as they do improving their tennis, golf, bridge, or gourmet cooking, the world of sales meetings, seminars, conventions, lectures, and luncheons would be a lot more enjoyable.

But, while there are thousands of good teaching pro's around to help you with your golf or tennis, there are few teaching humorists. While there are many books that offer bridge and cooking instruction, there are relatively few for laughter.

Here in one volume is a practical, workable explanation of:

1. Why people laugh
2. How humor works
3. What to do about it

Every chapter is filled with techniques for getting more laughs from the speakers platform.

If you've ever searched frantically through joke books and humor encyclopedias the night before a speech for something funny *and appropriate* for your audience or your subject, you'll appreciate the dozens of tips for getting the most out of a joke book in Chapter 4. You'll learn how to improve joke book humor by skillful editing, and how to classify and file jokes so you can find them quickly and easily when you need them.

If "telling" a joke effectively is ever a problem for you, you'll find much aid and encouragement in Chapter 1. You'll learn how to tell a joke because you'll learn how a joke really works, how it's constructed and why. You'll see how the component parts of a joke function to produce laughter. You'll learn what "timing" really means and how to do it.

In Chapter 6 you'll learn why a "sense of humor" is not something one has to be born with, but how it can be learned and developed as surely as one learns to swing a golf club or operate a typewriter. You'll also become acquainted with one of the top secrets of the professional humorist, the humor formula. You'll see how humor formulas make it easy for even a child to invent original gags and jokes.

Chapter 16 shows you one of the most valuable skills any student of any subject can acquire--how to learn how to learn. It shows you how to improve your understanding of humor and boost your laugh percentage through an effective and enjoyable program of humor testing and experimentation.

You often hear professional comics talk about "switching," the trick of turning old jokes into new jokes. Chapter 5 gives you a clear understanding of switching and shows you three switching techniques that work.

If you're one of those persons who believes that the highest purpose of humor is not the laugh, but the point behind the laugh, Chapter 14 shows you how to put humor to work to make a point. You'll learn how to use humor to clarify ideas and make ideas more memorable and persuasive. You'll learn how to convert a serious idea into a humorous idea without destroying its serious point.

Chapter 2 explains the reason behind the advice "different jokes for different folks." You'll learn how to analyze an audience to determine with professional insight what kinds of gags and jokes will make them laugh and why. You'll solve the mystery of why one person may find a joke uproarious while the next doesn't find it even slightly amusing.

This book does not aim to make you a professional humorist, but it will give you more practical, workable humor know-how than you can get from any other single source. While this book does not strive to make you a professional comic or gag writer, it will reveal more of their tricks and techniques than any other book ever offered to the general public. It will prove to you that "thinking funny" is no different than any other kind of thinking and that any intelligent adult can learn how.

Finally, this book will show you the way to an exciting new hobby. It will make you a student of one of the most fascinating and satisfying of all the arts, the art of producing that highly desirable, involuntary response known as laughter.

Bob Bassindale

ACKNOWLEDGMENTS

Hundreds of good people have helped me write this book. Some are mentioned in the text, many are not.

I thank them all, for the help, and for the laughs.

To avoid possible embarrassment to either the marksman or the target in much of the humor, names, occupations, occasions, and places have been changed or deleted.

Contents

1

How Speakers Learn to Tell Jokes

One of the oldest complaints in the English language surely must be—I just can't tell a joke. Obviously, successful platform humorists can. How do they do it? How do they stand up there and reel them off with just the right touch, just the right inflection and emphasis, just the right pause—or lack of pause? Can a person who can't tell a joke learn how? What does it really mean to "tell" a joke?

For one thing, it involves a lot more than merely making sure that you yourself get the point of the joke you're trying to tell. Failure to grasp the point of a joke can be disastrous for a speaker, of course. Even amusingly disastrous.

> An Englishman on his first trip to America went to one of those stand-up comic nightclubs for the first time.
>
> After he'd had a couple of drinks, the lights dimmed and Henny Youngman stepped into the spotlight and greeted the crowd with his famous trademark gag.
>
> Take my wife. Please.
>
> The crowd belly laughed. The Englishman was impressed. "By Jove," he said to himself, "I must remember that and try it on the chaps back home."

> Some weeks later, back in London, he stepped to the
> microphone at a meeting of his luncheon club and, with
> great confidence, snapped out . . .
>
> Consider my wife. Please.

Few speakers, British or American, would have bungled
Youngman's classic so completely. But there's a lot more to
successful joke delivery than merely remembering the right words.

Just what does public speaking talent have to do with telling
jokes? Everything. And nothing. Public speaking skills are vital to
the humorist. Joke telling demands skillful use of meaningful
emphasis, intelligent phrasing, and most other public speaking
fundamentals. But these don't constitute the real secret of the art.
I've never heard a funny speaker who wasn't a good speaker, but
I've heard many a good speaker who simply couldn't get good
laughs.

What about personality? Don't most humorous speakers have
likeable and interesting personalities? Yes, but so do many
unhumorous speakers. Larry Wilde, in his readable book *The Great
Comedians Talk About Comedy,* tells of an aspiring young comic
asking the great "Pro" Woody Allen about this very point. The
young man explained to Woody that just before he goes on stage
he tries to work himself up into a "happy" and "likeable" mood.
Woody's opinion? That's got nothing to do with it.

Well, if a likeable personality, public speaking skills, and the
mental capacity to "get the point" aren't the real secrets of telling
jokes, what are? They are a curious combination of profound
insights and clever tricks which nearly all funny speakers seem to
have learned by conscious or instinctive effort—and considerable
trial and error.

What Is a Joke Made of?

The majority of really amusing public speakers I have talked
with have a strong sense of what the professional comics and gag
writers call "joke construction." This "feel" for the component
parts and inner workings of humor goes beyond just getting the
point of a joke.

It not only helps speakers "tell" jokes more successfully, it
helps them in other ways. It helps them remember jokes better
because they have a better understanding of what it is they're

trying to remember and which parts are essential to the humor. This "feel" for joke construction helps them evaluate jokes and improves their ability to select jokes. It even helps them improve other peoples' jokes and invent new ones of their own.

What *is* a joke made of? Let's examine Henny Youngman's well worn masterpiece and see if we can find out. It *is* a masterpiece. Hidden in these four carefully chosen words is the secret of joke construction.

Take my wife. Please.

All the necessary parts are there. If we can understand this joke, we can understand virtually all of them.

Perhaps you don't find Youngman's joke to be your "style" of humor. Forget style for the moment. Style and construction are two very different things. A ranch house and a colonial mansion vary considerably in style. Room arrangement, decor and other styling features are quite different. But the component parts are much the same—bedrooms, bathrooms, kitchens, and so on—and the construction materials—the studs, bricks, shingles, and so on— are often identical. The same thing is true of humor. Styles and subject matter can vary widely—from slapstick to subtle, from literate to illiterate, from big city to small town. But the construction principles and component parts are remarkably similar.

The following, attributed to George Bernard Shaw, is regarded as one of the greatest sophisticated witticisms ever uttered. It was an exchange between Shaw and a famous ballerina.

> BALLERINA: Oh, Mr. Shaw, think what a perfect child we could have . . . with my body and your brains.
>
> SHAW: Suppose it had *my* body and *your* brains?

Compare its construction with this knee-slapper from the Grand Old Op'ry.

> BUMPKIN: My Grandpappy tried to cross a crocodile with a cucumber. He wanted to get a crock of pickles.
>
> STRAIGHT MAN: He can't do that.
>
> BUMPKIN: He found that out. All he got was a pickled croc.

The humor of London literary circles differs from the corn of the Tennessee hills much like a crepe suzette differs from a pancake. The taste may be different, but the construction is basically the same. But construction is all we're concerned about now.

One of the most unfortunate statements about the study of humor came, sadly, from a fine humorist—E.B. White. He said, "Humor can be dissected, as a frog can, but the thing dies in the process and the innards are discouraging to any but the pure scientific mind."

It's ironic that this much-quoted witticism has done so much to keep the practical study of humor in the dark ages. In their hearts, successful humorists know he's wrong. We're not looking for a scientific definition of humor—or a literary or psychological definition. We're searching for a *working* definition, something that will help a speaker learn how to tell a joke because it helps him understand what it is he is actually doing when he tells a joke.

A joke is a magic trick

When Henny Youngman says "Take my wife" he's doing exactly what a magician does when he rolls up his sleeves and shows the audience the hat is empty. When Youngman says "Please," he pulls a rabbit from the hat the audience thought was empty. A joke is a magic trick worked with words and ideas instead of mirrors, trapdoors, or secret compartments. Except a joke has one thing more than a typical magic trick.

Punch—A joke is a magic trick with punch

What's punch? That's not easy to pin down. Before trying to define punch, let's try to illustrate it.

If humor is a magic trick with punch, then we ought to be able to produce humor simply by adding punch to a magic trick. Sounds reasonable. Let's try it.

> Magician rolls up sleeves. Shows audience his hat is empty.
> Reaches in and instead of a rabbit . . . pulls out a *skunk.*

The skunk is punch. It's a little punch aimed at the audience. Let's aim some punch at the magician.

> Magician shows hat is empty. He reaches in, fumbles a bit, looks concerned, then angrily calls toward wings: "OK, wise guys, where's the damn rabbit?"

If that's too slapstick, we can refine it, make it more "David Niven" or "Rex Harrison" in its style.

> Magician reaches into hat, fumbles, removes empty hand, shrugs, and says: "Here I finally remember how to do the trick, but I forget the rabbit."

Ethnic punch is effective.

> Magician speaks with obvious Irish brogue and gives impression he's a bit into the gargle. He pulls a small leprechaun out of the hat.

> Black magician pulls rabbit's *foot* out of hat saying, "Ya don't *need* da whole rabbit, man."

Sex makes good punch.

> Magician reaches into hat and instead of a rabbit, pulls out a woman's bra.

How about some bi-partisan political punch?

> Magician is made-up to look like the President of the United States. He pulls a little man out of the hat who looks suspiciously like the Vice-President of the United States.

And sometimes we like our punch directed at mankind in general. At what the philosopher calls the "human condition."

> Magician is a giant rabbit. He shows hat is empty, then pulls out a small man.

These examples ought to give us a pretty good idea of what punch is. There are thousands and thousands of ways to convert the rabbit-in-hat trick into humor by adding punch.

Yet, there isn't 100 percent agreement among speakers on how to *define* punch. Depending on who you talk to they'll call it:

insult	poking fun	put down
ridicule	kidding	put on
criticism	conflict	sarcasm
truth	negative	etc.

So, take your pick, but we'll call it punch. It's a well-accepted word. Professional gag writers and humor editors talk about "punching up" a line or joke. And, no one seriously questions the meaning of "punch line." So, let's call it punch.

Regardless of what it's called it has to be there. Humor isn't humorous without punch. Without punch it's just a rabbit coming out of a hat. Surprising, enjoyable, but not funny.

But, take a surprise and add punch, or a punch and add surprise, and you've got humor.

Learning to Set Up an Audience

If a joke is a magic trick, it's logical to assume that a joke should be performed like a magic trick. The majority of the highly successful humorous speakers I've questioned agree that the first job the joke teller has is to mislead the audience to prepare them for the essential surprise of the payoff.

This part of the joke is the *setup*, and that's its function, to "set up" the audience with some verbal slight-of-hand. Henny Youngman does it by saying "Take my wife" as if it means "Take my wife, for example." Then, when we hear his punch line, "Please," we suddenly realize he didn't mean it that way at all. He meant, "Take my wife off my neck!"

One of the best ways to learn to appreciate the function of setups and to learn how to deliver them with the necessary slight-of-hand is to study them *before* you know what the punch line is. Let's try it. Doctor Walter C. Bornemeier, past president of the American Medical Association, has proved many times that he knows how to practice humorous deception as well as medicine. Here's the setup for a gag he used in a speech before the AMA's Woman's Auxiliary Board luncheon in Chicago.

> The first crisis this couple had when they were first married
> had to do with the usual one night a week out with the
> boys.

There's nothing funny about that. It happens to virtually every newly married couple. And the success of the gag depends on it being delivered just as it if *were* the usual, traditional newlywed debate.

Before glancing down at the punch line or payoff, study Dr. Bornemeier's setup carefully. Notice how innocent and reasonable it sounds. It's interesting, of course. It makes us want to hear more. But it's not funny. Yet!

Here's the payoff.

> He insisted that she give it up.

Is there any doubt that the success of Dr. Bornemeier's gag depends importantly on the deceptive attitude of innocence and even seriousness he assumes during the setup?

Let's examine another piece of humor in which the success of the payoff depends largely on the speaker misleading the audience with an innocent, reasonable attitude.

G.D. "Dick" Guy is the resident wit of the Waukesha, Wisconsin Rotary Club. If Dick hadn't chosen to make a success in the business world, I'm sure he could have made it as a comic or gag writer, or both. Here's an example of one of his hat tricks. He pulled it while mastering the ceremonies at his club's 50th anniversary affair attended by club members and their wives.

> It's fun to get dressed up for an evening out, isn't it? You girls walk into the dressing room and there you are, surrounded by sprays, lotions, perfumes, gay, bright-colored clothes . . .

Like Dr. Bornemeier's setup, this one seems to be an entirely reasonable and appropriate statement. It's pleasant, but not funny. Study it carefully. Now, look how beautifully it sets us up for Dick Guy's payoff.

> And that's just your husband's stuff.

Dick Guy creates much of his own humor. You can bet that when he gets up on the podium he doesn't destroy the sly deception he has carefully written into his setup by delivering it in a transparent manner.

The setups for gags like Dick's and Dr. Bornemeier's don't really need much more than a good poker face—a little "con artistry"—to give the audience the right wrong impression. Other gags need both a *deceptive attitude* and *special emphasis* on strategic words. These strategic words must be stressed because they must *connect* with a word or words in the payoff to communicate the surprising point.

A New York broker friend of mine is both a good golfer and a good talker. As a result he frequently wins trophies and masters ceremonies at his club. I won't use his name because he's publicity shy. That is, he's as publicity shy as a broker can afford to be. Here's an example of his humorous way with strategic words.

> People say women make lousy drivers. Not so. I've known
> women who could drive better than men.

It sounds like a sincere idea—so a sincere attitude ought to pull it off. But when we look at the payoff, we see how important the specific words "drivers" and "drive" are to the gag, why they must connect to make the point.

> But I've never seen one who could putt.

The connection between the ambiguous word "drive" and the payoff word "putt" must be made strongly to get a good laugh.

Here's another quip that demands strategic word emphasis in the setup. It's a favorite of a friend of mine who is in demand as a speaker at political picnics, where he eats his share of the food and gets his share of the laughs. He likes to start out with one like this.

> Boy, what a crowd! You know, there are an awful lot of
> people here.

His payoff works only if he puts strategic stress on one of those words. That becomes apparent when we look at his payoff.

> *Really* awful.

Unless the speaker hits "awful" in the setup, his "*Really* awful" doesn't work.

The late dramatist, George S. Kaufman, was famous for "doctoring" other people's plays, as well as for writing healthy ones of his own. A young writer once asked him for help, explaining that his play worked well up until the last act, then fell apart. Mr. Kaufman read the play, then explained, "The trouble with your last act is your first act."

The incident might easily have happened among humorists. An experienced comic might have told a beginner, "The trouble with your payoff is your setup." There is no question that when a speaker fails to put a joke across, the odds are at least even that he blew it in the setup, before he ever got to the payoff.

Why do so many speakers fail to recognize the importance of the setup to the laugh? Probably because setups aren't funny. Jokes are supposed to be funny. So apparently it seems logical to some speakers to concentrate on the funny part—the payoff. Speakers who get the laughs know better. They know the humor of the payoff depends almost entirely on the effectiveness of the setup.

Setups are not supposed to be funny. Their job is to set up the audience, to get it thinking clearly in the wrong direction, thus maximizing the surprise and the laugh in the payoff.

Learning to Make Payoffs Pay Off

If the setup of a funny joke isn't funny, surely the payoff must be. Right? Well, let's see. Here are some we've been working with.

> Please.
>
> He insisted that she give it up.
>
> And that's just your husband's stuff.
>
> But I've never seen one who could putt.
>
> Really awful.

It's hard to imagine any of these being even faintly humorous to anyone who hasn't been set up for them. They're just simple ideas, simply stated.

Let's study payoffs the same way we worked with setups, but in reverse—looking at the payoff before we know the setup.

One of the country's wittiest speakers is also one of the country's finest football coaches, Hugh "Duffy" Daugherty of Michigan State. Duffy's retired from coaching now, but not from making people laugh. Here's the payoff for one of my favorite "Duffyisms."

> . . . by my enthusiasm.

This doesn't look any more amusing than a setup. You're

probably thinking only a genius could make those three words funny. And here is Duffy's ingenious setup.

> The trouble with you Alumni is that you get carried
> away . . .

Let's examine another Duffyism. Again, we'll take it back-yards, payoff first.

> He's a senior.

Again, it's hard to imagine anything less amusing, by itself, than this payoff. But you can be sure Duffy Daugherty didn't depend solely on the payoff for his laugh. He was careful to precede it with this.

> He is a great football player . . . with just one weakness.

By now, you're probably concluding there really isn't much difference between a setup and a payoff. You're right. It's the *connection* between the two that creates the humor. This idea suggests that many jokes could be told backwards. As a matter of fact, one of the more successful gag formulas is the "backward gag." Johnny Carson uses them for his Great Carnack routine. Steve Allen also is fond of the backward gag. Here's one of his best. I liked it so well I've remembered it for ten years or more.

> The answer is . . . for shooting down 15 Messerschmitts.
> What's the question?
> Why was Hans von Stumpf kicked out of the Luftwaffe?

This basic joke, originally written backwards, can be easily reversed and turned into a forward gag with just a few revisions.

> Henreich, haf you heard? Von Stumpf has been kicked out
> of za Luftwaffe. Vy, dot man shot down 18 planes.
> Ja. But 15 of zem were Messerschmitts.

If setups and payoffs are so often interchangeable, what is the difference between them? Order. Order of delivery. The setup comes first. They are two halves of a whole. Each half has the capacity to explain or reveal the other half. So, whichever comes first will be revealed by the other.

By themselves, payoffs are usually just as innocent, mislead-ing, pointless, and unfunny as setups. And, the best ones are written so the revelation doesn't come until the last word or two. Concentrate on this idea of the *revelation*. It's the most important part of the gag. Another look at the payoff for the out-with-the-boys gag shows how deceptive a payoff can be until the revelation.

Here's that payoff *without* the revelation.

He insisted that she give it

Give it what? Her approval? Her consideration? Until the last word, "up," there is no real revelation. And until "up," the best delivery of this payoff is exactly like that of the setup, with meaningful but deceptive emphasis. But "up" must be given clear emphasis. This doesn't necessarily mean it must be shouted with Shakespearean bravado or other cornball histrionics. Often emphasis comes from a lack of conscious emphasis. Before you decide that this is nonsense, try delivering this payoff like this.

He *insisted* that she *give it* up.

This is one of several effective ways to deliver it. But, "up" must come through. It must be clearly audible. And, until a speaker has developed true finesse in the subtle shades of emphasis, he's on safest ground if he delivers a setup like this with definite stress on the revelation.

He *insisted* that she give it *up*.

Stress the revelation. That's the best advice for anyone trying to improve his or her ability to tell jokes.

> *Please.*
> He insisted that she give it *up.*
> And that's just your *husband's* stuff.
> But I've never seen one who could *putt.*
> *Really* awful.
> by *my enthusiasm.*
> He's a *senior.*

The revelation is what pulls it all together and explodes the laugh. The safest technique is to give it the strongest emphasis of anything in the entire gag.

If a joke is just a string of misleading, deceptive information with a sudden revelation, why divide gags into setups and payoffs?

Why not into setups and revelations? Many gags are basically that. They're called one liners, like this one from William H. Roylance's *Complete Book Of Insults, Boasts And Riddles.*

You should go to work for Maytag as an agitator.*

But even a one liner like this may work a little better if there's a slight pause inserted to break it into setup and payoff.

You should go to work for Maytag . . . as an agitator.

This is bordering on "timing" which is another important ingredient in the delivery of a joke.

How Speakers Learn Timing

The timing of comedy can be a very difficult art. Comics, directors, and actors sometimes work hours to get just the right timing into a piece of comedy, especially visual comedy. Fortunately, the timing of the kinds of jokes, gags, and stories most suitable to public speaking is a much less difficult, much less complicated thing.

If a joke is told *too fast,* the audience won't be surprised because they won't understand enough of the gag to be surprised. They won't get the necessary misleading information. If a joke is told *too slowly,* two disasters may occur. The audience may simply drift away, lose interest, and forget the strategic misleading information in the setup. They're not surprised by the ending because they don't remember the beginning. Or, the audience may start to figure the joke out ahead of time, resulting in no laugh at all or a scattering of little laughs that interfere with the main laugh.

So, the first principle of good timing is to:

Tell the joke slowly enough so the audience gets a good, clear, misunderstanding, but fast enough so it doesn't lose the thread or start to catch on too early.

How fast is too fast and how slow is too slow? That decision

---

*From the book, *Complete Book of Insults, Boasts, and Riddles* by William H. Roylance. © 1970 by Parker Publishing Co., Inc. Published by Parker Publishing Co., Inc., West Nyack, New York.

is largely a matter of combining judgment, good public speaking technique, and a feeling for joke construction. I said I'd never heard a funny speaker who wasn't a good speaker, and one of the important things a good speaker brings to humor is a sense of timing. A good speaker senses when he's going too fast or too slow by watching his audience carefully, watching their faces to make sure they are interested and that they understand step-by-step what he's saying.

Obviously, there are two major ways to keep them interested and "with it." Both are a matter of emphasis. One is by stressing certain words. The other is by pausing after key points to let them "sink in."

This pausing is 90% of the mysterious thing called "timing." A speaker who can deliver a serious line like this with good timing,

> I have a general, uneasy feeling that our company is confusing strategy with tactics.

should have no trouble timing a quip like this,

> I have a vague, unfounded, unjustified suspicion that other people think I'm paranoid.

A speaker who can "time" a Shaw epigram,

> Take care to get what you like or you'll end up liking what you get.

should feel comfortable timing a quip like this,

> He's really something. He has the strength of a rabbit and the speed of an ox.

The same thing applies to longer pieces of humor. Let's examine Dick Guy's "dressing up" story alongside a nearly identical serious idea.

It's fun to get dressed up for an evening out, isn't it?	It's fun to go to the Grand Canyon, isn't it?
You girls walk into the dressing room.	You park your car and walk down a rocky path hewn out of stone.
And there you are!	And there you are!
Surrounded by sprays, lotions, perfumes, gay, bright-colored clothing.	Standing on the rim of creation.

| And that's just your husband's stuff. | And that's just the beginning of the adventure. |

There's no excuse for anyone who can bring good "timing" to the serious Grand Canyon material not being able to "time" the Guy gag equally well. The same principles are involved. The word "beginning" performs the same function in the serious payoff that the word "husband's" does in the joke, and so on through the entire story.

Most, though not all, of what's called "timing" in joke delivery is simply effective use of pace, pause, and word inflection for meaning and emphasis—techniques that are common in serious speaking. Why don't more laugh-seeking public speakers realize this? Undoubtedly the idea of performing humor throws them. They get uptight. Stage fright and anxiety get in the way of common sense. I can't promise that this information will make you a flawless joke timer, but I will promise you this much. If you make a serious effort to understand the principles of joke construction and humor psychology covered in this book, you'll be amazed at how much your "timing" will improve.

The reason your timing will improve is that with a better understanding of how the joke works you'll be better able to bring to it the emphasis and communication techniques that *any* important material must have, whether it's humorous, merely amusing, or deadly serious. The timing of *comedy* is a horse of a different hue. But, fortunately, the public speaker doesn't have to use comedy to get good laughs.

The Raconteur Versus the Comedian

I have questioned hundreds of outstanding humorous speakers about performing comedy and acting funny on the speakers platform. Seventy-five percent *never* do it. They play the role of a "raconteur" or reporter of humorous ideas. They "pass along" or "share" humorous material with their audience. Of the remaining 25% who *do* use some comic talent delivering humor, only a handful do it most of the time.

In other words, somewhat over 97% of the outstanding humorous speakers I have surveyed say they can get good laughs without trying to act funny. Even the ones who can and do use comedy technique tend to use it carefully and sparingly.

The great golf pro, Lee Trevino, for example, has a fine talent for comedy and does use it. But he also offers this sobering advice.

Usually, the best way to tell a funny joke is . . . seriously.

Jim Gillie of Phillips Petroleum Company is often compared to Will Rogers. Mr. Gillie does "very little acting." Most of the time he says his delivery is "straight, calm, and deadpan, with smiles only where they are clearly appropriate." And, Jim Gillie warns, "Never milk the audience."

Milking the audience is one of the hazards of trying to act funny. When you simply relate humorous ideas to an audience there is a healthy climate of "take it or leave it" prevailing. But when you try to act funny, you'd better succeed because the audience knows for sure you are working at the job of trying to get a laugh. Once an audience gets the idea you're really trying to make them laugh there's a danger they will try to resist your temptation. A laugh is built up and released. Only a talented comedian can force it.

What are these comic talents so many successful speakers avoid?

Funny faces. All of our faces are funny to some people. But the skill of assuming a truly comic expression on purpose eludes most of us. And, it isn't necessary, not even for professional comics. Unconvinced? Make the "silent screen TV test." Tune in Johnny Carson or some other outstanding comic during a monologue, but turn the sound off. Don't listen. Just watch. You'll be amazed at how seldom you'll see anything you could call a funny face, or even a broad grin. You'll be hard pressed to believe they're delivering funny material at all.

Funny voices. Some of us have naturally amusing sounds to our voices—pinched, nasal, gutteral, or other qualities—and some of us don't. Some who don't have it naturally can achieve it. If you can't, don't try.

Funny accents. Some of us talk naturally like a Bronx cop, a European immigrant, a Chicago mobster or a Tennessee squirrel hunter. Some of us have learned how. If you haven't, don't try it until you do.

Funny gestures. We all use body language. But some people can express themselves very comically with gestures and other bodily movements. Again, if you can't, don't.

Unless a speaker is absolutely certain he has the natural or learned ability to look funny, sound funny, talk funny, or move funny, he'll do himself and his audience a favor by being:

Witty rather than wacky.

Psychologically funny rather than physically funny.

A raconteur rather than a comedian.

2

How Speakers Learn
What Jokes to Tell

It's hard to say which is least appreciated by an audience, a bad joke well told or a good joke poorly told. When an experienced humorist is on the platform the audience seldom has to make that choice. He not only knows how to tell jokes, he knows how to pick them.

This doesn't mean any speaker can bat one thousand with humor. There's no such thing as a surefire joke or a guaranteed laugh. But the really successful speakers seem to get a much higher laugh percentage. It's not so much that they get louder laughs, they just get more of them. They don't bat a thousand, but they're usually way above five hundred.

How do they do it? How do they seem to pick just the right gags on just the right topics with a much greater frequency than less amusing speakers?

For one thing, most of them make no effort to act funny or perform comedy; they're careful to select material that doesn't require it. Material that's on the humor, rather than the comedy side of the funny line.

How do speakers distinguish humor from comedy?

Avoiding the Comedy Trap

There are some long, dreary, and debatable dissertations on the question of humor versus comedy. They're fine if you're preparing for a career as a drama critic or taking a Ph.D. in Balzac, but they're not very helpful to the public speaker.

There *are* some practical guidelines. They come from people who are *getting* laughs, not just *theorizing* about them.

Is it funny on paper? That is, does it read funny to the eye when it's written down? Or do you have the uncomfortable feeling that to put it across you'll have to play the role of a funny character, use a funny accent or try to say something serious in a funny way? Comedy material often doesn't read funny at all on paper. That's because comedy often depends more on the way the material is handled rather than the material itself. For the humorist, the material is usually the whole show and it should read funny . . . even scribbled on the back of an envelope.

Is it difficult to say or pronounce? Most humor not only reads funny to the eye, it flows easily off the tongue. Comedy, on the other hand, sometimes requires extremely fast delivery or tongue-twisting.

Does it contain dialogue? Dialogue doesn't automatically make it comedy. But it's a warning sign. Whenever a joke or story has a lot of "he saids" and "she saids" it may actually be a very difficult comedy routine disguised as a joke. Whenever a joke depends importantly on dialogue, a wise speaker studies it carefully to make sure it can be put across without winning an Oscar for character acting.

The difference between humor and comedy isn't *always* critical. But the further a joke falls beyond the comedy line, the more probable that its success depends on theatrical talent.

Here are two good examples of humor that absolutely demand comic delivery. They come from Seymour Kleinman, a prominent Manhattan attorney and professor at Columbia Law School, who is both a great humorist and a gifted performer.

What a strange country, America! Before I came here, would you believe it, I didn't have an accent.

It's pointless told straight, in American lingo. But do it as Sy can do it, in a believable, well-tuned ethnic accent of almost any kind—German, French, Yiddish, Italian, Russian, Chinese, for example—and it takes on great meaning and makes a penetrating comment on human vanity.

His second example also demands a foreign (non-Irish) dialect. It's great, for example, as a Yiddish story.

> What a wonderful country, America. I came here an immigrant boy without a penny. Today . . . a partner in a flourishing firm. Schwartz and McCarthy.
>
> Where except in America could you have such a firm? And on the best of terms. Never a harsh word between us.
>
> And I got for you a further surprise.
>
> I'm McCarthy.

Stories like these should never be attempted by any speaker who is tone deaf to the beautiful music of the so-called "foreign" accent. In jokes like these it is the accent that makes the point. However, there are many other types of dialogue jokes, filled with opportunities for dialect, slang, and other colorful speech, which do not rely on these verbal tricks to make their point. While they're usually funnier if told with authentic speech, they can be done successfully by any capable speaker who follows the basic rules of humor delivery. A speaker doesn't have to avoid phrases like "Good old boy" in southern jokes and "Youse guys" in gangster gags merely because he doesn't have theatrical skills. He can handle such lines easily and casually without fear of destroying the point of the humor.

Many good dialogue jokes contain *no* challenging character roles. The dialogue is logical and conversational and needs only logical and conversational delivery to make it work. The following story, one of the all time classics, makes no real comic demands on the speaker, yet it is loaded with dialogue.

> Three newly deceased candidates for heaven sit in the waiting room of St. Peter's office.
>
> Finally, St. Peter returns from lunch and asks the receptionist to send in the first candidate.
>
> "How did you die and why do you think you're eligible for heaven?" St. Peter asks.
>
> "Well," says the man, "For some time I suspected my wife was cheating on me. This morning a neighbor called and

confirmed the awful truth. He told me a guy had entered our apartment a half hour ago and hadn't come out."

"Furiously I rushed home, burst into the apartment, and found my wife lying naked on the bed.

"I started to search the apartment in a jealous rage. I looked through the whole flat ... under the bed, in the closets, behind curtains ... everywhere.

"I found no one. Finally, out of sheer frustration and blind rage ... I picked up the refrigerator, carried it out onto the back porch, and threw it down into the backyard, three stories below.

"The exertion and excitement must have been too much for me. I must have died right then and there of a heart attack."

"Well," said St. Peter, "That's a very unusual way to die, but entirely moral. Admitted. Send in the next candidate."

The second candidate told an even more surprising story.

"St. Peter," he said, "If you'll excuse the expression I swear to God I was minding my own business taking a nap in a hammock out in the backyard. I heard a noise and looked up just in time to see a full sized refrigerator falling on me from the third floor."

"Hummmm," said St. Peter. "Most tragic and most circumstantial. But, again, entirely proper and moral. Admit this man and send in the next candidate."

"St. Peter," said the third candidate. "I know you're not going to believe a word I say. I just know it. I got called to this lady's apartment to fix her refrigerator. I was working on it when all of a sudden she screamed, 'Here comes my husband, for God's sake hide!' So help me, St. Peter, the last thing I remember was climbing into that refrigerator and closing the door."

Notice that none of the four people in the joke, not the three candidates for heaven or St. Peter himself, require any difficult characterization. No dialects, lisps, or any other difficult comic touches are needed. This doesn't mean a speaker shouldn't give them some interesting personality dimensions if he has the ability, but it's not necessary to put the joke across.

So, the first rule in selecting the right jokes is to choose material that fits your talent, or lack of talent.

The second rule is to fit your material to your audience.

Learning to Analyze an Audience

The speakers who get the laughs owe their success in part to their ability to fit their material to their audience. And they usually rely on some kind of conscious or instinctive audience analysis to accomplish this.

Why does analyzing an audience help a speaker select successful jokes? Aren't funny jokes funny to everyone? Hardly. Funny jokes not only aren't funny to everyone, their funniness varies from time to time, from occasion to occasion, and from audience to audience.

To fully understand why this is so, it's helpful to understand the true function of a joke. Earlier we defined a joke for the benefit of the joke teller. We said it was a magic trick with punch. Now, let's try to define a joke for the benefit of the joke selector, for the benefit of a speaker trying to decide what jokes to tell.

Instead of describing how a joke is constructed, as we did before, let's try to describe what it does and how it functions.

A joke is a device that makes people laugh at people

Putting it another way, people don't laugh at jokes, but at other people. A joke is merely a device that causes them to do that. So, when trying to select a joke that will be funny to a specific audience, a speaker is really trying to select a device that will make the audience laugh at someone.

Every joke has a butt. Or, as some of us prefer to call it, for fear of being misunderstood, a target. A joke is a surprising punch or charge of ammunition fired at the right target. If the shot catches the audience by surprise, and if they approve of the ammunition and the target—if they think the "punishment fits the crime" so to speak, they'll laugh.

Sometimes the audience is so anxious to laugh at the target the speaker selects, the joke doesn't have to have much more than punch.

I see Ed Jones is here, looking hung over, as usual.

With another audience, or at another time, the speaker may

have to use more deception to get more surprise into the gag—to literally surprise the audience into overcoming its natural inhibitions.

> I see Ed Jones is here. Ed, you look just like you looked ten
> years ago. Hung over.

But in either case, Ed Jones must be a good target—someone the audience is anxious, or at least willing, to laugh at. And, the accusation "hung over" must be the kind of punch the audience will permit the speaker to throw at the target.

Julian Frazin, a very successful Chicago lawyer and chairman of the Chicago Bar Association's annual political comedy show, is often asked to emcee and humorize political banquets and similar events. Once he was called on to say a few amusing and appropriate words at a dinner honoring the governor of Illinois.

At the time, the governor was involved in a heated political debate over the merits of building a cross-town expressway in Chicago. Regarded as somewhat of an interloper among old line Illinois Democrats, the governor had gotten elected on an economy platform. He was taking the "taxpayers part," he said, in opposing the cross-town expressway.

The governor happened to be about a half hour late to the dinner. When he arrived, Mr. Frazin, hit by what he calls an inspirational flash, the kind of inspirational flash that comes often to humorists of Mr. Frazin's caliber, explained the late arrival this way.

> The governor wishes to apologize for being late. You see, he
> had a little trouble getting . . . cross town.

In the words of show biz habitues, it broke the joint up.

Mr. Frazin hit on exactly the right ammunition for exactly the right target at exactly the right time for exactly the right audience. This is what makes the humor of public speaking as strategic as chess and as exciting as pro football. It's a game of wits in more ways than one. The speaker must be witty with his humor. But he must also use his wits to choose the right humor for the right audience. And trying to figure out this little puzzle is largely a matter of selecting the right target and choosing the right ammunition.

Selecting the Right Target

The president of a firm is having some minor but well-publicized differences of opinion with the Internal Revenue Service, and is about to be introduced to make a few remarks at a company party. The senior vice president, a long time friend of the president, gives his boss this witty little welcome to the podium.

> Our next speaker needs no introduction. What he does need
> is a good tax attorney.

The roof blows off. Why? It's a clever dig, to be sure. But why the mass belly laugh?

Actually, the success of the gag is due far more to the choice of target than to the cleverness of the wit. The target is the boss. The vice president gave the audience a sudden chance to laugh at their boss. And that's something most people secretly want to do. It was primarily the strength of the target that powered the laugh.

People like to laugh at anyone who holds a position of authority over them. At bosses of all kinds, even at immediate supervisors. At government officials–local, state, and national. At police officers. Even at people who hold semi-authority like ministers, teachers, civic leaders, and club officers. At anyone who's in charge of things. People also like to laugh at anyone they suspect is smarter, better looking, luckier, or richer than they are.

We can lump this whole target group together as *superiority figures.* Experienced speakers know that an audience enjoys laughing at most people they regard as superior in any way.

An audience also likes to laugh at people they regard as their inferiors. These *inferiority targets* include people we think are less intelligent, less attractive, less sophisticated than we are, or whose occupation, religion, culture, national origin, or race we regard as inferior.

This psychological phenomonon operates in obvious ways in so called dumb jokes, ugly jokes, fat jokes, ethnic jokes, and racial jokes. But it operates in much gentler, much subtler ways in good natured gags like this little quip from a Baptist minister addressing an outdoor ecumenical conference on a cloudy day in Indiana.

> Well, the weatherman hasn't done us any big favors today.
> But . . . this weather isn't bad. It's certainly plenty good
> enough for Methodists.

It's an extremely light jab but the audience eats it up for the same reason other audiences go for "Polish" jokes.

People can have some farfetched reasons for regarding other people as their inferiors. And, those feelings of superiority can be strong or weak. But whether the feelings are farfetched, strong, or weak, inferiority figures make good humor targets.

Who else do people want to laugh at? At any of their associates who are likely to disturb their peace, quiet, self-esteem, or self-indulgence. This list includes wives, husbands, kids, in-laws, neighbors, friends, acquaintances, competitors, and many others. We can call these people *conflict targets*.

A marriage counselor looks seriously at his audience and says:

> I can't understand why so many people have trouble getting
> along with their mother-in-law. I'm very fond of mine.
> There's nothing I like better than taking my mother-in-law
> out for a nice drive. To the airport.

Unfairly or not, the mother-in-law is one of the prime targets on the conflict list, not because she is superior or inferior, which she may be, but because she is so frequently a source of conflict. The best explanation for the continuing popularity of mother-in-law jokes is the probability that the great majority of married people suffer conflicts with either one or both mothers-in-law.

But, if you're a mother-in-law, or especially fond of yours, don't feel too bad. As a conflict target, the mother-in-law is only a little ahead of wives, husbands, divorced mates, kids, other in-laws, neighbors, and many other competitors.

So, the wise speaker tries to select gags that have strong targets—some person or group that members of the audience think of as superiors, inferiors, or as a source of conflict. Making the game even more interesting is the fact that some of the best targets fall into more than one category.

A not-too-bright boss becomes both a superiority and an inferiority target. A minister, priest, or rabbi can be both a superiority target because of position, and a conflict target because of his constant moral reprimands. A political figure can be both a superiority target because of his election victory, but an inferiority or conflict target because his political views or affiliation doesn't please you.

But, to qualify as a good target, as someone an audience is particularly anxious to laugh at, a person or group usually falls into at least one of these three categories.

Here's a little game that can open your eyes to the strategic importance of humor targets. Substitute various other people or groups for "wife" in Henny Youngman's favorite gag.

> Take my brother-in-law. Please.
>
> Take my broker. Please.
>
> Take the guy who fixed my car last time. Please.
>
> Take the guy who sold me these shorts. Please.

Any substitution you make that makes the line funny for you is probably a good superiority, inferiority, or conflict target for you.

The speaker has a big advantage over the professional comedian when it comes to selecting targets. The comedian faces a nightclub or TV audience with a bewildering assortment of occupations, educations, backgrounds, interests, hangups, and prejudices. It isn't easy to pick hot targets for such a varied group. The comedian is almost forced to attack very *general targets* such as widely known public figures and personalities, unknown or fictitious people against whom he can fire strong ammunition. Often, the comic must "build up" the target to get the audience feeling strongly about it before he actually goes into the gag.

> I worked for a guy once who was really stingy. Boy, was this guy tight with a buck. He was so stingy . . .

The public speaker usually faces an audience that is far more uniform in occupation, education, and other characteristics. Often as not, they're nearly all members of the same club, employees of the same company, members of the same sex, or have the same marital status. As such, they share a strong desire or willingness to laugh at *specific targets,* far more than does a typical night club or TV audience.

A speaker talking before a large group of salesmen can attack district sales managers, knowing that almost everyone in the audience feels strongly about them. The comic, whose audience may be half housewives and one in which only a few of the men are salesmen, can't rely on such specific targets.

And so it goes throughout the world of public speaking. The more uniform the audience, the easier it is to select especially strong targets. Despite this, many inexperienced speakers have a talent for choosing poor targets to shoot at.

The Worst Targets—and the Best

There probably are only two really bad target categories.

Sacred cows are probably the most obvious bad targets. There aren't many of them. There aren't many people whose accomplishments, stature, or reputation make them immune to an audience's desire to laugh. But some speakers seem to seek them out with almost a self-defeatist instinct.

But there's another risk target that inexperienced speakers seem to attack with even greater frequency. The audience itself. Despite all the folklore about what good sports we all are and how well we can "take a joke," most of us would rather laugh at just about anybody but at ourselves.

Some speakers may try to get an audience of women to laugh at women instead of such an easy target as men. These ill-advised marksman will also try to make corporate tax attorneys, for example, laugh at corporate tax attorneys instead of at, say, internal revenue people. A speaker who tries to get an audience to laugh at itself is bucking the odds. It can be done, but it's getting a laugh the hard way. One way to get the job done is to share the punch with the audience.

An Indianapolis investment counselor, discussing stocks and bonds before a group of doctors, opened his talk with this quip. Notice how it punches both the doctors and the speaker.

> It's such a pleasure to be able to talk to a bunch of doctors
> for a change without having to take off my clothes.

This brings us to perhaps the safest and handiest target of all, the speaker himself. Nine out of ten of the outstanding speaker humorists I've talked with say they pick on themselves much of the time. Why?

For one thing, who's going to resent it? The speaker's mother? She's seldom in the audience. Secondly, the seasoned laugh getter knows it helps him win over an audience. They accept him as a good sport who doesn't take himself too seriously. Thirdly, it earns a speaker the permission, in a sense, to pick on other targets. Most audiences seem to follow an unwritten code that a speaker who is willing to kid himself has the right to kid others.

One of my favorite speakers, a California manufacturer's representative, is a master at this.

> I know you'll be surprised to hear this, but my wife has a serious drinking problem. Me.

After punching himself in the nose like that a few more times, he opens up on his friends and their friends with no fear of turning any of them into enemies.

This last gag and the quip about nudity during visits to doctor's offices, brings up the point that it isn't always easy to be sure who *is* the main target of a joke. If the drinking gag is told fairly straight, the speaker becomes the main target. If, however, the speaker says "Me" with some real enjoyment, conveying the impression that perhaps one of the reasons he drinks is to aggravate or get even with his wife, then the wife becomes the main target.

Some gags seem to have no target at all to the untrained eye.

> Chicago has a very good climate . . . but lousy weather.

Who does this joke punch in the nose? It's admittedly indirect, but remember, we don't laugh at cities or weather, we laugh at people. I'm sure you'll agree that this gag punches lightly at the Chicago Chamber of Commerce and at any other super-patriotic Chicagophiles the audience may be acquainted with.

Before leaving targets and moving on to ammunition, let's deal briefly with one objection you may be raising to the theory that we laugh only at people. What about animals? Why is Donald Duck funny? Why do you occasionally laugh at your own dog or cat?

Projection, or, as the psychologists call it, anthropomorphism. We project human personalities, motives, likes, and dislikes on to animals and, because of this projection, can laugh at them as if they were people. It's not a terribly important point, perhaps. Few speakers concentrate on funny animal stories. But, if you do, just make sure you "humanize" them in your stories. You'll get a better laugh.

But most humor has a human target, and a fairly obvious one at that. And, selecting that target is half the job of fitting your humor to your audience. The other half of the job is just as important, and, perhaps, more difficult.

Choosing the Right Ammunition

The ammunition or punch of a joke must be chosen with as much care as the target. The punishment must fit the criminal and his crime, and the audience is the judge of all three—criminal, crime, and punishment. We can see this more clearly by switching targets and audiences for a couple of gags we used earlier.

Let's pretend that Ed Jones' lodge is having the outdoor meeting on the cloudy day instead of the ecumenical church group, and that the emcee uses the same ammunition against Ed that the Baptist minister had fired against the Methodists.

> Well, the weatherman hasn't done us any favors today. But . . . this weather isn't really bad. It's plenty good enough for Ed Jones.

Chances are the joke just won't make it. The ammunition isn't up to the target for this audience. For the audience, it's like watching pro football players in a game of touch football.

And, suppose the Baptist minister speaking before the church group used lodge hall punches against a different Jones. Unnecessary roughness!

> This is a wonderful religious experience. It's so good to see so many old friends we haven't seen in a long time.
>
> Like Reverend Jones. You know . . . he looks just like he looked ten years ago. Hung over.

You don't often find speakers mis-matching targets and ammunition as obviously as we've done in these overdone examples. But less obvious mis-matches occur frequently, usually to the detriment of both the laugh and the speaker's reputation. If you laughed at the "hung over" ammunition being fired at the minister, remember, you are not a member of that audience. An audience usually doesn't want a speaker to obliterate a target, just hit it.

Some speakers use bullets of such excessive caliber that they're like a six-foot father punching his seven-year-old son in the jaw for common disobedience. A scolding or spanking, okay, but a punch in the jaw? But small caliber ammunition usually isn't very funny. It doesn't give the audience sufficient reason or excuse to laugh at the target.

How do speakers learn to walk the tight rope when choosing humorous ammunition? How do they pick punches that are neither too weak nor too strong? One way is to make sure the joke is *clever.* Experienced speakers know that cleverness usually takes the sting out of ammunition that otherwise would amount to inexcusable insult.

Chicago publisher Robert Oelrich knows what cleverness can do to help make sure a target and an audience will accept his punches without resentment. In addition to being a talented humor hobbyist, Bob Oelrich has been a finalist in the Toastmasters International humorous speaking contest. Here's one of his favorites.

> This girl isn't the greatest cook in the world. Her husband
> bought her a foreign cookbook. But she can't use it. She
> says she can't get the parts.

It's unlikely any woman or audience would resent such witty ammunition. Comparing foreign cooking with foreign cars is a genuinely clever idea. It's a painless way of accusing a woman of being something less than a great cook.

A wise speaker avoids choosing ammunition that is merely unmitigated gall. He looks for gall that is mitigated by clever wit. Instead of calling a business associate stupid, he finds a clever way to suggest it, as in this gag a banker used while criticizing some of his associates for being naive about modern business techniques.

> Some of them still think public relations means having
> intercourse out in the street.

They say humor is the soul of wit. Most certainly wit is an effective insulation against the shock of humorous insult.

Another way to make reasonably certain your audience will

accept the punches you throw at your target is to follow Dick Guy's advice and use such obvious untruth or exaggeration that your audience will know beyond any doubt that you're just kidding.

Here's a beautiful example of the Waukesha humorist's *obvious untruth* technique in action.

> Joe was a star basketball player in high school. He also was listed on the honor roll for getting three grades of 90 or better and none below passing.
>
> That was great, Joe.
>
> What went wrong?

The target, of course, is a very successful, well-liked man. Nothing has gone wrong. It was an obvious case of just kidding.

But, a speaker must make sure he's throwing such ammunition at the right target. Aiming the same punch at someone who had indeed suffered some misfortunes or serious problems would have violated the sense of "fair play" almost all audiences seem to have. It would have gotten a cool reception.

Another way speakers stay in that middle ground of not too timid and not too tough is to choose ammunition that is gutsy enough to survive the "just kidding" climate and still have some punch left. Certain kinds of punches are better than others at withstanding joking and kidding without withering. We might call these punches *gut ammunition.* They include sex, elimination, stupidity, ugliness, dishonesty, cowardice, and other human functions, characteristics, and defects that seem to stir the emotions of an audience more easily than others. Obesity falls into this category.

At a recent shareholders meeting a genial fat man asked a question from the floor. The executive conducting the meeting was discussing another point so he asked the fat man to hold his question for a moment. Only he did it this way.

> Dan, would you mind sitting on that question for just a minute?
>
> On second thought, Dan, you'd better not sit on it. Just hold it in your hand.

It got a terrific laugh. Not so much because of the wit but because the target was really fat and fatness is one of the gut punches. This gut ammunition is so powerful, a speaker can handle it very lightly and cleverly and still end up with plenty of punch.

There's another way of fitting ammunition to a target, one that may seem to be a bit of a "cop out." But it has permitted many a speaker to salvage a good joke he might otherwise have thrown away.

Change the Target

If you have a story or gag in which the ammunition is clearly too strong or too weak for the target you had in mind, change targets.

A Kansas City salesman who likes to borrow jokes from nightclub comics couldn't wait to use this gag in a sales convention speech.

> This guy was a real loser when it came to sex. Nothing worked for him. Finally, in desperation, he sent away for one of those sex instruction record albums.
>
> Even that didn't work. The album was recorded at 33 1/3 and his turntable only goes at 78.

He got into the middle of his speech and was about to use the gag with a particularly sensitive associate as the target, thought better of it, and told the joke on himself instead. He got a laugh, and kept a friend. If you find funny ammunition that doesn't seem just right for the target you had in mind, don't waste it, switch targets.

Up until now we've been talking about choosing a punch that is emotionally right for the audience and the target. Effective ammunition has to *communicate* too. The audience has to understand it.

Some ammunition doesn't communicate because it's *too vague*. A highly successful woman executive in San Francisco likes to tell what it's like for a woman to get to be a vice president in a man's world of business. Here's one of her favorites.

> People ask me about the problem of sex in the business world. It's there. But you can deal with it.
>
> Once I had to attend an out-of-town convention with a department head. I was to make the hotel arrangements. He suggested that we . . . ah . . . have . . . adjoining rooms.

> I got them adjoining all right. I put him in 1647 . . . and I
> stayed in 1547.

It's a good laugh getter. But it wasn't always. Originally, she
told it this way.

> . . . I got them adjoining, all right. Vertically.

It was logical, but vague. She communicated the idea much
faster when she substituted the vertical room numbers for the idea
of "vertically." You often hear people say they like "subtle"
humor, but nobody likes vague humor.

Sophistication is another potential road block to humorous
communication. This quip was used before an extremely intellectual audience at Yale by an extremely intellectual speaker.

> Did you hear about the artist who found a cure for his
> insomnia? At bedtime . . . he'd have some hot rococo.

They laughed. But it can only be funny to people who know
and care what rococo means.

Here is an equally sophisticated story which is equally
unsuitable for any but a very sophisticated audience, in this case,
financially sophisticated. It comes from Seymour Kleinman. He
got a great response with this gag from a staff reunion of the
Securities and Exchange Commission.

> The board of directors of a corporation met to consider
> some very dire financial problems.
> The president said, "Gentlemen, we have a choice. Either
> we go public . . . or we go bankrupt."
> The chairman said, "We have no choice. We must go public.
> There's too much disclosure in bankruptcy."

It's a side-splitter when told to a sufficiently sophisticated
audience. And, as Mr. Kleinman points out, it's very sophistication
is a compliment from the speaker to the audience. Incidentally,
Mr. Kleinman has a sly "I.Q. test" that he gives an audience before
he uses any of his sophisticated material. He'll open with an
intellectual quip like this.

> You'll notice that a good deal of my material is in dialect.
> Matter of fact, my kids call me a dialectical materialist.

If he gets an appreciative chuckle from one like that, he

knows he can use sophisticated and intellectual humor with that particular crowd. This "test" is an indication of how carefully a really accomplished humorist tries to fit his ammunition to his audience.

Until a speaker has learned to judge an audience as shrewdly as Sy Kleinman, he's well advised to avoid subtle, sophisticated humor. Remember, it isn't necessary to be sophisticated to get laughs. Laughter comes primarily from our emotions, not from our intellect. Many jokes and quips titillate the intellect, but their humor depends primarily on the extent to which they stir the emotions. You can never get an unsophisticated audience to appreciate sophisticated quips, but many an intellectual audience has laughed uproariously at very unsophisticated material.

How Long Should a Joke Be?

The "refrigerator" joke told earlier in this chapter is 364 words long. It takes as long for an audience to listen to that joke as it does for them to watch three one minute television commercials. Henny Youngman's "Take my wife" has only four words. Think about that and you'll understand why most successful platform laugh getters use short gags and short stories. As Oklahoman Jim Gillie puts it, "Stay with short stories and one liners so if they fail it isn't traumatic." Imagine taking three full minutes of an audience's time to tell a joke they don't like? The longer a joke or story is, the funnier it had better be.

There's another good reason for this growing interest in short humor. The length of a piece of humor seldom has anything to do with how funny it is. Speakers know that with shorter gags and quips they can get more laughs per minute. Why waste two or three minutes of a speech to get just one laugh with one lengthy story when in the same time span you might get four good laughs with four short quips?

Learning to "Die" Gracefully

Most speakers who have developed the ability to get good laughs got the talent by having the *courage to fail.* They learned how to "die" with dignity and to profit by it. It is neither a painful nor a permanent death.

If a speaker plays the role of a reporter or "passer along" of amusing ideas, if he doesn't put himself out on an embarrassing limb by trying too hard to "make" his audience laugh, why should silence or even a small groan wound him painfully?

If the speaker is seriously interested in learning more about the fickle art of getting laughs, he knows that every failure may contain a valuable lesson. When a speaker does his homework, chooses the right target and effective ammunition for his audience, then delivers the setup and payoff with reasonable skill, and still doesn't get at least an appreciative chuckle, he's had a valuable learning experience if he'll only take the trouble to analyze it.

It may be that, despite his efforts to find fresh material, that particular audience may have heard that one before, too many times before. The audience may not have been in the mood for the gag. The immediate mood of an audience can be influenced by a number of things, most of them beyond the control or even the awareness of the speaker. And, sometimes the mood of the audience simply overpowers the skill of the speaker and the quality of his humor. For example, it's always easier to get a laugh from an audience that has had something to drink, but it can be more difficult to get a laugh from an audience that has had too much to drink. The audience may be under some unusual tensions or pressures the speaker has no inkling of. A speaker, after all, can analyze an audience just so far. He can determine who they want to laugh at and what will usually make them laugh under average circumstances, but he can't often analyze what they had for breakfast.

I know of one talented speaker who showed up at a sales convention in New York with enough good material to wow a salesman audience. What he didn't know was that the hotel where the convention was being held had infuriated most of the audience the night before by making a shambles of room reservations, rates, and other supposedly pre-arranged details. By nine o'clock the next morning they still were in no mood to laugh at the material the speaker had prepared. Had the speaker known this, he might have come up with a few aggressive "bad hotel" jokes. But he didn't know it. And that's an example of one of the breaks of the game.

What about "savers" and other gags professional comics use when a joke bombs? They're fine, if you're willing to memorize some good ones and are sure you can put them over. Frequently such material is more difficult to deliver than the gag that failed in the first place. The best thing for the average speaker to do when he doesn't get a laugh is to grin and shrug it off, and learn from it.

3

Discovering the Three
Great Sources of Humor

Learning to select good jokes won't help much if a speaker doesn't know how to turn up a good assortment to choose from. Through the years, I've asked many outstanding witty speakers where they get their humorous material. The answers may or may not surprise you, depending, I guess, on any preconceived notions you may have.

More than 80% of those queried use *original* humor at least part of the time. Sixty-five percent *borrow* jokes, gags, and stories and use them pretty much "as is." Their sources are fairly obvious, friends, acquaintances, newspapers, magazines, books, TV, and radio. Sixty percent engage in humor *remodeling* or *editing*. They take old jokes or other borrowed humor, and through rewording or restructuring turn it into a better version of the same joke, or into an entirely new joke that to the untrained observer may not appear to have any connection with the original.

These figures add up to more than 100% because the great majority of speakers make use of more than one of these sources. About a third of them use all three.

To me, the most surprising thing about these informal statistics is the high degree of creativity. It takes original thought to edit, remodel, or invent humor. Ninety-eight percent of these speakers perform at least one of these functions in preparing their speeches. Remember, of course, that the survey was taken among speakers with established reputations for getting laughs. Had we included any speaker who occasionally tries to get a laugh, I'm sure the incidence of originality would have been much lower. This is not to discredit humor that is borrowed verbatim. If a gag or joke is worded effectively when a speaker finds it, no experienced speaker will change it just for the sake of change.

The Great, Unofficial Humor Lending Library

We're using the term "borrowed" humor because of the amusing reply a speaker friend of mine gave to another speaker who had accused him of stealing his jokes.

> I never steal jokes. I just borrow them. After I use them, I always return them to their original owner . . . usually in much better condition than when I took them.

There *is* a great humor lending library out there. It's never closed on Sunday. You don't need a library card to use it. And there are no fines for overdue jokes.

Finding jokes isn't the problem. Finding appropriate ones is. Like professional comics, successful speaker-humorists know that out of every 100 jokes they run across, perhaps no more than half a dozen will be appropriate for their speech. Typically, a large number of the jokes are pure comedy—just for laughs. And, whether the audience is white, black, brown, red or yellow, many of the jokes will be too blue.

We haven't discussed so-called off-color humor and we won't, except for these points. First, it generally follows the same principles of construction and laugh psychology as clean humor. Second, a smart speaker doesn't use it unless he's pretty sure of himself and his audience. A speaker should never delude himself into thinking that an off-color joke that goes over big in a bar with an audience of five or six people will be similarly received by an audience of 350 who haven't had anything to drink. But our society seems to be getting more permissive by the month, and it would be wrong for a speaker to assume that he must prudishly avoid any implication of sex or elimination in his humor.

Here are some samples of lightly spiced humor that speakers have used with great success before very "polite" and "proper" audiences.

> It's possible to be absolutely paranoid on the question of marital fidelity. The other night at a party a friend of mine walked up to a newly married young swain and said... "Say, I think your wife is terrific." "Yeah," said the groom, belligerently grabbing him by the lapels, "How do you know?"

> Courtin' as we know it seems to be a thing of the past. I know a guy and a girl who have been going together for seven years. She keeps turning down his proposals. Like the other night he said, "For the 900th time ... will you marry me?" She said, "We'll talk about it in the morning... c'mon let's get a little sleep."

> Someone has asked the arrangements committee if they will serve watermelon at the annual picnic. I've told them that's OK with me as long as they check first to make sure that the road home has plenty of filling stations.

Notice that none of these quips contains any so-called dirty words. They could be told with safety to most audiences, including many church groups.

The decision of whether to use these jokes is largely a matter of a speaker's personal lifestyle and judgment. But, to categorically exclude two of the most powerful laugh producers in the arsenal, reproduction and elimination, is to rob humor of much of its fun and earthy human interest.

Many jokes a speaker runs across must be ruled out because the ammunition doesn't fit the target. As we discussed earlier, you can't use "Ed Jones" ammunition against a "Rev. Jones." And, general irrelevancy takes a heavy toll. Much of the humor a speaker turns up cannot be made to fit the topic of his speech no matter how ingeniously he tries to lead in to it, lead out of it, or even explain in detail why he told it.

When the entire collection has been strategically and tastefully screened, a speaker is very happy if as many as five percent of the gags he knows are of any use to him for any specific audience. So, he knows he must have a lot of jokes available in order to assure himself of just a few that are right for the occasion. He needs quantity to assure quality.

One of the most important differences I've noticed between laugh producers and yawn producers on the speakers platform is the way the former take such pleasure in *collecting* humorous material. They make a virtual hobby of it.

What *are* the best sources of borrowed humor? "Heard any good jokes lately?" That may be a good way to start some small talk with a friend but it apparently isn't a prolific source of humor, judging by the answers given by the speakers in my survey.

Surprisingly, fewer than 20% of them make important use of friends, relatives, acquaintances, business associates, and other social contacts. There are some good probable reasons for this. Most people we meet casually haven't heard any good jokes lately. Furthermore, most of them can't remember the ones they have heard, and the ones they do happen to remember seldom fit a speaker's purpose.

There are some exceptions. One of the wittiest talkers on the big time banquet circuit has developed a small but loyal army of friends who act as humor scouts for him. They know exactly what kind of material he wants and they pass along anything that passes muster.

Other speakers purposely seek out people who do hear good jokes and remember them. They'll even invite such good joke sources out to lunch just to pick their brains. One in particular is so adroit at this that he confesses he never wastes valuable time telling his guest any of his own jokes. He just collects the other guy's.

Another speaker collects jokes the way folk singers collect folk songs, by stopping in small towns on vacation or business trips, and chatting with the legendary and witty old timers he goes out of his way to meet.

So social gatherings, chats, bull sessions, and other informal, person-to-person get togethers *can* produce good material. But you have to work to get the material.

By far the most important source of borrowed humor for the speakers in my survey is the printed page, that is, newspapers, magazines, and books.

For example, everyone knows the *Reader's Digest* has a lot of amusing, witty, and funny stuff in every issue, but not everyone realizes what a truly fantastic and prolific source of humor it really is. An average issue contains more than 100 pieces of short humor, ranging from homespun to sophisticated. When a speaker goes to a good library that carries maybe 20 years of back issues, he's got thousands of jokes to choose from in this one remarkable publication. Not only that, the *Digest* publishes compilations of its best humor in book form, which makes it even easier to get at.

Parade magazine, formerly published by one of our humor experts, Arthur "Red" Motley, runs a weekly column of the favorite jokes of professional comics. Most of these have not been widely used on TV. Thus, *Parade* provides more than 500 good gag ideas a year.

Many so-called "trade" or professional magazines carry good humor.

Small town newspapers can be an excellent source. Some are; some aren't. A little digging is needed to find the good ones, but the effort is worth it. If a speaker can make friends with some humor-minded small town editors, he may be able to tap into a humor grapevine. Most of them exchange their publications for other small papers around the country. The result is a clearing house of thoughtful and humorous homespun material. Much of this stuff has a "Will Rogers" style to it, and some of these local editors approach the great Oklahoma humorist in ability to comment wisely and wittily on the passing scene.

Another source of humor in print, a not-so-obvious source, that can serve the public speaker well is the one panel cartoon. Many of the gag lines are largely "verbal" in their humor despite the fact that they have picture attached.

> I won't say this is a cheap restaurant but there are only two
> beans in the three bean salad.

The wide world of one panel cartoons is filled with gags like that. They take only the slightest editing to fit into a speech and get a good laugh.

The many joke books and humor encyclopedias in book stores and libraries are under-rated by most inexperienced speakers. They are far more useful than many speakers realize. These books vary in type and style of humor depending on the talents, interests, and taste of the author. A wise speaker examines every new humor book that comes out to see how closely it fits his ideas of what's funny and what's appropriate.

Some of these volumes concentrate on illustrative stories and point-making jokes. The many fine anthologies by Judge Jacob M. Braude and Herb V. Prochnow are particularly good. Others, like those by Joey Adams, Bob Orben, Leopold Fechtner, and William H. Roylance, lean more toward gag-insults. Most of the humor in these collections is more aggressive.

Both types of humor books are very useful to the speaker who knows how to get the most out of them. Many speakers don't. We'll learn more about how the experts exploit these books in future chapters.

We've touched on only some of the many places a speaker can go to borrow humorous material for his speech. The fact is, humor is everywhere for the speaker who keeps his eyes and ears open to it, but it must be collected systematically and methodically to be useful. And "collect" is the right word for it. The wittiest speakers I know make a real hobby of it.

There's another good reason for a speaker to collect jokes—even bad jokes.

The Workshop Where Old Humor is Rebuilt

Some of the best jokes used to be some of the worst jokes. That is, they were bad until some speaker saw something promising in them and turned them into relevant, up-to-date material.

This process of taking an old joke or a poor joke, tearing it down and revising or rebuilding it into a better joke or even a totally new joke, is something most talented humorists learn to do sooner or later. It's the next natural and logical step after a speaker develops a real feel for the construction and psychology of humor.

Some of it consists of joke *editing.* Joke editing is something nearly all talented speakers do to make a joke or quip fit their delivery better or fit into their speech more fluently and meaningfully.

But some of it goes way beyond simple editing. It becomes a real rebuilding job in which a basic joke is completely disassembled, new parts are added, and it is reassembled into a totally new piece of humor. Professional comics and gag writers call this *switching.*

Our survey of outstanding speakers shows that more than half of them depend on joke editing and remodeling much of the time. We'll examine editing and remodeling in more detail in the next two chapters. But, for now, here's an example of the remodeling process in action.

A sociology professor at a Midwest university looked for a joke to help him convince an audience of women that their influence over men is much stronger than they suspect. He came up with this one, which he got by frankly and unashamedly remodeling a joke told by one of America's wittiest clergymen, Bishop Fulton J. Sheen.

Here's the gag as the sociologist told it.

> I don't think the average woman has any inkling of what a strong influence the so-called weaker sex has on the so-called stronger sex.
>
> The other day I was standing in the checkout line of one of those super drug stores.
>
> The woman behind me asked if I'd mind if she moved ahead of me in the line.
>
> Noticing that the only purchase she had was a hairbrush, I said, "By all means. Ever since childhood I've had an enormous respect for any woman with a hairbrush in her hand."

Now, here's the original as Bishop Sheen told it.

> Recently, on the subway, I got up and gave my seat to a lady who was holding on to a strap.
>
> She was rather surprised and said to me, "Why did you do that?"
>
> Seeing that she was incapable of understanding a spiritual reason, I said to her, "Madame, I tell you, ever since I was a little boy, I've had an infinite respect for a woman with a strap in her hand."*

---

*From the book, *The Wit and Wisdom of Bishop Fulton J. Sheen* by Bill Adler, Editor. © 1968 by Bill Adler. Published by Prentice-Hall, Inc., Englewood Cliffs, New Jersey.

The basic funny idea here, that a grown man who was spanked in childhood will respect a woman who holds any instrument of discipline in her hand, can be the basis for a number of different jokes.

This remodeling job looks fairly obvious because we are examining both the original and the rebuilt gag side by side. In actual speech making practice, it is rare when an audience stops to examine a gag and to think of some joke that might have been the original model.

Joke remodeling and editing is so prevalent it has understandably led to the frequent conclusion that there is no such thing as original humor. In a sense this is true. It's probably impossible to invent a piece of humor today for which one cannot find some structural or psychological precedent. But so what? The man who invented the game of roulette owed a great debt to the original aborigine who invented the wheel, if you want to look at it that way. Anyone who works in the various fields in which creativity and imaginative problem solving are important, knows that most if not all new ideas are merely new combinations or new interpretations of old ideas.

The Think Tank Where Original Humor is Invented

If it surprised you to learn that eight out of ten of these successful laugh getters get a good portion of their laughs with original humor, it may surprise you even more to learn how they go about it.

One of the popular myths is that people who create original jokes don't know how they do it. Only 12 percent of our surveyed speakers fall into that class. Only about one out of ten says he just seems to have a knack for it. This doesn't seem to have any effect on the quality of their humor however. One of the most delightfully witty woman business executives in the country freely admits that she has no idea why audiences find so many of her comments and observations so amusing. She just seems to look at the world through funny colored glasses.

We all know people like this woman. The interesting thing is that among a select group of outstandingly successful platform humorists they should constitute such a small minority. Thirty-five percent of our speakers fall into what might be called the "think funny" crowd. They have developed the ability to study current events, interesting situations, and other aspects of life that appear to have only a serious side to most people, and come up with amusing interpretations or suggest humorous consequences.

A St. Louis lawyer is particularly good at spotting serious stories in the newspapers and then thinking funny about them. Here's an example of the way he works.

> I saw in the paper the other day that some scientists have established communication with dolphins by learning their language of squeaks and grunts.
>
> When the communication breakthrough came, I understand the first thing the Dolphins said to the scientists was, "Don't you guys have anything better to do than sit around and shoot the bull with us?"

It's what we might call a technique where the humorist lets current events write his setup for him while he uses his imagination and his humor to invent a payoff.

Marshall C. Lewis, vice-president of American Can Company, is another speaker who has taught himself to think funny. Mr. Lewis says he tries to think absurd or opposite to find the funny side of serious things. He believes it is a way to test the validity of a viewpoint.

Here Marshall Lewis punches deftly at his own field of public relations, at liberals, conservatives, and many others in a speech at a public relations awards dinner in Chicago.

> I've come to the conclusion that the best training for public relations work is to grow up on the south side of Chicago.
>
> When I was a kid on the south side we had an image problem . . . and we didn't even know it.
>
> Today, it's regarded as "socially responsible" and liberal to live in an integrated neighborhood.
>
> Here we were, liberals without knowing it.
>
> I know of one south sider who figured the best thing for him to do was to change his name and move to the suburbs.
>
> All of you who are "accredited" members will recognize that as a much recommended public relations technique . . . change your name and move to the suburbs.

Incidentally, Mr. Lewis' reference to "accredited" members was a dig-within-a-dig. The field of public relations, like many others, has engaged in much introspective, self-regulatory activity. Marshall Lewis, thus, fired a double barrelled shot at public relations people in general and at the accreditation movement in particular.

Thinking funny is an art. But like most other arts it can be learned, up to a point. Not all of us can learn to think funny as quickly and fluently as a Marshall C. Lewis. But all of us can improve our ability.

With some 12% unsure of their methods, and 35% in the think funny school, how do the other successful laugh getters originate humor? The rest, more than 50%, make conscious and systematic use of humor formulas and techniques.

What are humor formulas and techniques? They are established patterns and maneuvers that can be used to achieve successful humor, just as football patterns and maneuvers can be used to gain yardage on the field. Humor formulas and techniques don't guarantee a laugh all by themselves anymore than football plays guarantee a score or a first down. Both have to be executed properly. But once a speaker learns to understand and use some of the most effective humor formulas and techniques, the job of creating original humor suddenly becomes an enjoyable game rather than the complete mystery it is for most people. Humor formulas and techniques are so important to the education of a humorist, we'll be devoting several chapters to them later in the book.

Planned Versus Ad Lib Humor

If there is myth and mystery surrounding the creation of original humor in general, there is even greater confusion and questionable folklore in the specific field of "ad lib" humor. Make no mistake about it, there *is* such a thing as ad lib humor. Ad libbing itself is not a myth. It happens all the time.

Two of the best quips earlier in this book were ad libs: Julian Frazin's crack about the governor of Illinois and the cross-town expressway, and the suggestion by the chairman of the shareholder's meeting that the fat man not "sit" on his question. Both of these were great spur of the moment originals.

But these and most other successful ad libs are *reactions* to something that was said or done unexpectedly. If the governor had not been late, Julian Frazin might never have thought of the cross-town crack. If a thin rather than a fat stockholder had stood up to ask a question from the floor, the chairman might never have had the occasion to come up with his deft fat gag.

Experienced speakers know that it's almost impossible to predict when the opportunity for an ad lib may pop up. So, they don't go into a speech planning to ad lib. They don't depend on ad libbing because they know they can't depend on ad lib openings and opportunities.

If a waitress should happen to drop a trayful of dishes and the speaker has the presence of mind to think of it, he may come up with something like this.

> When I heard those dishes break, I thought for a moment
> my wife was here.

But the humorist doesn't depend on ad lib humor. He knows that ad lib humor is usually uninformative, unpredictable, unreliable, and unworthy of the great concentration and preoccupation it requires. A speaker who goes through a presentation constantly thinking of ad lib possibilities probably doesn't spend enough time thinking of the planned portions of his speech to do a good job.

Most effective speaker humor is planned. It may be scribbled on a menu or a cuff at the last minute before a speaker is introduced. It may never be written down at all. But most of the funny stuff that serves a purpose on the podium is well planned in advance.

The most informative comment on ad libbing I've ever heard came from a politician friend of mine who is quite good at it. He said he never used to be able to ad lib anything funny. But, for that matter, he never used to be able to think up anything funny in advance. When he learned how to do the latter, he said, he was amazed at how his talent for the former improved.

Moral: The best way to learn to come up with something funny *on* the spur of the moment is to learn how to come up with something funny *before* the spur of the moment.

4

Making Other Peoples'
Humor Work for You \

There's an old but helpful saying which is sometimes used to judge advertising ideas.

Is the idea working for you, or do you have to work for it?

Some ideas seem hardworking but actually fail to earn their keep. They take more than they give. The same thing can happen with humor. A joke or gag may seem appropriate, but when the speaker tries to fit it into his speech he finds he's working for it instead of vice versa. It comes across contrived or forced or fuzzy.

Talented public speakers know how to make humor work for them. They learn how to use humor as a tool instead of becoming a tool of their humor. The methods they use to accomplish this control come into play at virtually every stage of the preparation of the speech, from the moment they begin to evaluate a joke right up to the time they polish the final draft or outline of their talk.

Learning to Evaluate Borrowed Humor

When an inexperienced speaker looks through a joke book he usually has only two things on his mind: funniness and subject matter. He's looking for a joke he thinks is funny, and he's looking for a joke that deals with the subject matter of his talk. If he's going to talk on agriculture, he looks for a "farmer" joke.

Most experienced laugh getters take a far more professional approach. They look first for the *point* a joke can make. The point it makes obviously, or the point it can be made to make with proper interpretation or editing.

Consider entry #1431 from one of the most successful joke books ever published, *10,000 Jokes, Toasts & Stories* by Lewis and Faye Copeland.

> An elder farmer was moodily regarding the ravages of the flood.
>
> "Hiram," yelled a neighbor, "Your pigs were all washed down the creek."
>
> "How about Thompson's pigs?" asked the farmer.
>
> "They're gone too."
>
> "And Larsen's?"
>
> "Yes."
>
> "Humpf!" ejaculated the farmer, cheering up, "Tain't as bad as I thought."*

A well-known economist used this story—not primarily because it's amusing, not because it's about farmers or pigs or floods, but because it so beautifully helped illustrate an important point he was making about how emotions and circumstances play a significant role in the attitudes people have toward economic hardships.

Because he chose the joke for its point-making capacity, see how adroitly he was able to blend it into his speech.

> No matter how much we talk about it, we keep losing sight of the tremendous *human* factor in economics.
>
> Remember the story of the Arkansas farmer who was wiped out by a flood. Totally dejected, he sadly looked over his soggy and battered acreage.
>
> "Hiram," a neighbor told him, "Your pigs are all washed down the creek."

---

*Two jokes from *10,000 Jokes, Toasts & Stories* by Lewis & Faye Copeland. Copyright 1939, 1940 by Lewis and Faye Copeland. Copyright © 1965 by Doubleday & Company, Inc. Reprinted by permission of the Publisher.

"What about Thompson's pigs?" the farmer asked.

"They're gone too."

"And Larsen's?"

"Down the creek."

"Humpf," said the farmer. "Tain't as bad as I thought."

The fact is, man is willing to endure much hardship if he knows he's not the only one suffering. If he knows he's not the only one whose pigs are down the creek.

You'll notice the speaker did some adroit editing of the joke itself. We'll discuss editing a little later. For now, let's concentrate on the point a joke can make, its illustrative capacity, and the memorability it can bring to an idea or an opinion.

Why do we stress the importance of the point of a joke? Because this is really the main reason most good speakers use humor in the first place: to make a point, to give an idea greater clarity, and to make the idea more vivid, more memorable, or more persuasive. So, doesn't it seem sensible for a speaker to concern himself first and foremost with the point a joke can make when he starts to judge its usefulness to him?

Sometimes the point a joke can make comes out of the situation or the occasion, rather than out of the topic of the speech. Picture a master of ceremonies starting to introduce a speaker following a particularly bad lunch—a real peas-and-carrots catastrophy. Aggressive feelings are running high in the audience. They want revenge. They want someone punched in the nose, figuratively speaking—the chef, the arrangements committee. Someone. Anyone.

If our emcee is a systematic joke collector he's got some good "bad food" gags on tap, like this one on page 66 of William H. Roylance's *Complete Book of Insults, Boasts and Riddles.*

This is food for thought. It's certainly not for eating.*

With a little quick editing, it comes out like this.

I'm sure our speaker this afternoon is going to give us some good food for thought.

*From the book, *Complete Book of Insults, Boasts, and Riddles* by William H. Roylance. © 1970 by Parker Publishing Co., Inc. Published by Parker Publishing Co., Inc., West Nyack, New York.

> I'm awfully glad. The chef sure as hell didn't give us any
> good food for eating.

The value of the gag lies almost entirely in its being delivered
in the right situation. As a gag, all by itself, it's a mildly amusing
little play on words. As an appropriate, aggressive comment
following a spectacular culinary failure, it has the capacity to
release strong laughter.

This brings up another reason why seasoned speakers use
point-making humor. It's funnier. When a speaker uses humor to
say something important or appropriate, to illustrate a dull or
difficult idea, he improves his chances of getting a laugh. He
increases the likelihood that the audience will both understand the
point *and* laugh at the joke.

This is understandable if we remember our earlier discussion
of audience laugh resistance. People often resent a speaker's
efforts to "make" them laugh. When the speaker uses an illustrative joke or gag, it is obvious to the audience that the main
purpose of it is not the laugh but the illustration. The audience
senses this. It lowers their laugh resistance. Thus, a joke becomes
funnier when it becomes relevant.

This peculiar piece of audience psychology is so powerful it
can even make a very old and worn joke successful. Experienced
speakers know that the appropriateness of a joke often has more
to do with its success than does its age or even its familiarity.

I once heard a speaker discussing a particularly embarrassing
and hopelessly scrambled corporate problem with some fellow
executives. It was the proverbial can of worms, in the full sense of
that cliche phrase. A real jumble of who-did-what-to-whoms.
Everyone had some egg on his face. The speaker got a great laugh
merely by reminding his audience of only the punchline of an old,
old joke—one we've already talked about.

> Really, I'm beginning to feel like the guy trying to get
> into Heaven and telling St. Peter, "So help me, the last
> thing I remember was climbing into the refrigerator and
> closing the door."

If he'd tried to tell the same story to the same audience on a
less relevant occasion they would have stopped him fast. But, on
this occasion, the great relevancy of the story made even the

punchline alone fresh and funny. It's a great "victim of circumstances" story.

So, the main thing a speaker who really knows how to use humor effectively looks for as he browses through a joke book is not how funny they are, but the point they can make. And he doesn't limit his attention to the obvious point. He studies the joke thoughtfully for other possible angles, analogies, parallels, and applications.

These thoughts should suggest to the beginner a whole new way to read a joke book, a whole new way to look on any humor you run across.

Classifying Humor for Strategic Use

Experienced speakers who use humor systematically have the opportunity to label or classify jokes and stories in advance, according to the kinds of ideas they can illustrate and the points they can make. Then, when preparing for a speech, they can locate the kinds of humor they need with relative ease.

Classifying jokes according to the points they can make isn't really difficult for anyone who understands the practical psychology of getting laughs. But it does take study and concentration. For example, how would you label the "lost pigs" story? The point the economist extracted from it, that suffering is easier to take when it's shared with others, is not the kind of thing that fits neatly on a file divider tab. An experienced speaker would probably classify it under four quick and short headings: suffering, hardships, jealousy, and competition.

Here's another joke that can serve many different illustrative purposes in a speech. It's #168 from *Braude's Treasury of Wit and Humor.* How should it be classified?

> A bunch of chickens was in the yard when a football flew over the fence and landed in their midst.
>
> A rooster waddled over, studied it, then said, "I'm not complaining girls, but look at the work they're turning out next door."*

---

*From the book, *Braude's Treasury of Wit and Humor* by Jacob M. Braude. ©1964 by Prentice-Hall, Inc. Published by Prentice-Hall, Inc., Englewood Cliffs, New Jersey.

Let's agree at the start that to classify this only as a "chicken" joke or a "rooster" joke would be to seriously misunderstand the function of humor in public speaking. This is not to say that it might never be used to good advantage by a speaker who wanted a good poultry story. The gag can indeed make a point about raising chickens. But that's not its most likely use. To develop its most exploitable point-making abilities a speaker must do some imaginative musing and pondering.

What about the football angle? Does it have any application to football? That's possible. A coach might chide his running backs like this:

> The way you guys keep fumbling I have to assume you have no respect for the football.
>
> A football is an impressive object. It should be treated with respect.
>
> Remember what the rooster said when a football landed in the chicken yard . . .

Not bad. But it has a much broader commentary to make.

A company president might use it in a talk to his district sales managers.

> Remember, not all sales incentive programs depend on monetary reward. Some of the best are based purely on an appeal to the salesman's pride.
>
> Remember what the rooster said when the football flew over the chicken yard fence . . .

A union official might use it to attack what he thinks are transparent and unfair tactics by management to increase worker production.

> They keep handing out this crap in little booklets telling us how proud we ought to be to break our backs for the company.
>
> It reminds me of what the old rooster said the day that a stray football landed in the chicken yard . . .

A women's lib speaker might use it to illustrate male chauvinism.

> We keep calling them male chauvinist pigs. We ought to call them male chauvinist roosters.

> Like the rooster whose flock of hens were surprised one day by a football that happened to land in the chicken yard . . .

And, a male chauvinist might use it for the opposite purpose.

> The best way to handle women was clearly demonstrated by a rooster one day when a football happened to land in the chicken yard . . .

A politician might use this same story to attack opponents he believes favor excessive military expenditures.

> They keep telling us what an awesome arsenal our enemies have.
>
> The facts don't back them up. I think they're too easily impressed by any strange missile they happen to see.
>
> They remind me of the chickens who were suddenly surprised by a football falling into the chicken yard . . .

And, there are many more possibilities.

If this one story can do all these things and more, how should it be classified for handy reference and use? In his book, Judge Braude puts it under the heading of competition. But it also could be advantageously labeled incentive, motivation, leadership, male chauvinism, female gullibility, stupidity, xenophobia, and many others.

If Judge Braude and other writers and compilers of humor encyclopedias were to give every joke all of its possible strategically useful labels, they would have room for only a handful of jokes. Most of the book would be taken up by classifications.

The job of classifying good jokes according to the many illustrative uses they have is clearly the job of the speaker. In my entire collection of joke books, for example, there is only one index reference to incentive. Yet incentive is a subject that comes up frequently in public speaking, especially in the business world. There are hundreds of good jokes in these books that can make one point or another about incentive.

Look through the table of contents and index of some of your favorite humor anthologies. You'll see they don't have many references to the kinds of points and ideas public speakers most often want to illustrate. You'll find a lot of people references: wives, husbands, mothers-in-law, uncles, bosses, politicians, and so on. You'll find a lot of location references: New York, the Bowery, Chicago, Chinatown, hick towns, Niagara Falls, Grand Canyon, and so on. You'll find a lot of general topic references: sex, marriage, vacations, jobs, secrets, flying, swimming, and so on. But you don't find many references to such basic human issues and problems as jealousy, laziness, vanity, misunderstanding, poor sportsmanship, greed, impulsiveness, dishonesty, cleverness, or even something as common and relevant as plain everyday stupidity.

For example, one of the most popular joke books, a massive work with thousands of good gags and stories, compiled by a professional gag writer, contains only one reference to stupidity. Yet there are hundreds of great stupid jokes in the book.

This limited indexing is one of the reasons why so many speakers don't find joke books and humor encyclopedias as useful as they might. The humor simply isn't organized and labeled in a useful manner. Experienced speakers don't let this stop them. They organize their own humor collection or joke file to suit their own work methods. They classify the humor according to the topics, subjects, and ideas they deal with most frequently in their speeches. It's not as big a job as you might think, especially if you love good humor and enjoy working with jokes for a few hours every week in much the same way other hobbyists work with their collections.

A Humor Filing System That Works

A simple, practical, efficient joke filing system permits a speaker to work at the job of classifying humor in his spare time so that he can easily pick the right joke for the right point when preparing a speech. There's no one right way to do it, perhaps not even one best way to do it, but the following system fills the prescription for a method that's simple, practical, and efficient.

First, the jokes are filed on cards by number—your own numbers. You don't worry about different numbers for certain kinds of jokes. This isn't like the Dewey decimal system.

You simply take a card, 3 x 5 is the most practical size because any joke that can't go on both sides of a 3 x 5 card is probably too long to tell anyway, and put your own number at the top and the joke in its original form on the card. Don't bother to change it, just get it down on the card the way you heard it or found it in a book, magazine, newspaper, or other source.

It's as simple as this:

> **138**
>
> "But Madame, you have no claim. Your husband did not insure his life. He took out a policy against fire."
> "That's what I claim. He has been cremated."*

This joke, incidentally, happens to be #2706 from the Copeland's *10,000 Jokes, Toasts & Stories.* But we don't worry about *their* number. *Our* number is 138. And that's all there is to the *filing* of jokes. The rest is *indexing.* That means filing according to classification, of course.

The first classification that comes to mind here is "stupidity." There are many others, but let's start with stupidity.

We take another 3 x 5 card and label it "stupidity" across the top and enter our joke number, 138, on this index card. It's likely that several earlier jokes will have also been indexed for stupidity, so our card probably looks something like this.

> STUPIDITY
>
> 1   19   40   41   87   103   138

And by the time our file gets up into the thousands of jokes, our "stupidity" index card is probably covered with numbers on front and back because stupidity is one of the most frequently occurring ideas in both jokes and speeches.

This index card is then filed alphabetically.

Thus, the joke filing system consists of two files of 3 x 5 cards. The jokes themselves are labeled and filed by number. The points, topics, and subjects are filed alphabetically.

Our next step is to develop further classification of the same basic gag.

---

*Two jokes from *10,000 Jokes, Toasts & Stories* by Lewis & Faye Copeland. Copyright 1939, 1940 by Lewis and Faye Copeland. Copyright © 1965 by Doubleday & Company, Inc. Reprinted by permission of the Publisher.

For a woman to try to collect on fire insurance because her husband was cremated is either dumb or smart depending on interpretation. It also could represent dishonesty. So let's enter joke #138 on two more index cards labeled "shrewdness" and "dishonesty."

Studying the joke some more, shifting our point of view from the main character, the widow, to the insurance man, for example, we see that the joke could serve as a wacky illustration of "salesmanship." It's not inconceivable, from a comic point of view, that an insurance salesman sold her the fire insurance policy on the basis that she could collect if her husband were cremated. And because "marketing" is closely related to "salesmanship" we could also file it under that heading. And, obviously, we could also file it under "insurance" and "widows" and "death" and "funerals" and, of course, "cremation."

Where should we stop? If we just let our imaginations run wild we'll end up with a simple joke file and a monstrously complicated index. At this point the speaker's judgment and knowledge of his most likely subjects and topics comes in. He indexes jokes only according to his needs. And, there's another natural deterrent to excessive indexing. Many jokes don't lend themselves to dozens of different classifications.

> Anytime you think you're neglected, just think of Whistler's father.

This crack by James Montgomery Flagg is well-indexed under "women's liberation," "neglect," and "father," and possibly "inferiority complexes."

> In politics . . . some men are self-made but most are machine-made.

To file that one under anything but "politics," and "self-made" is probably impractical.

So, even though some jokes and stories can be indexed all over the place, many of them, and most of the short quips, lend themselves to no more than four or five.

Joke filing, then, is a simple matter of filing the jokes numerically and indexing the several different points or ideas they can illustrate alphabetically.

Once securely filed and indexed, a good joke is ready to use in a speech, except one more process is needed. Editing. What is joke editing and why is it necessary?

Secrets of Successful Joke Editing

In many ways the editing of jokes is no different from the editing of business letters, memos, news stories, speeches, and other written material of a serious nature. It can vary all the way from minor changes in punctuation and word order to extensive rewriting and major overhauling.

Is humor editing really necessary? If a joke has proved to be a laugh getter with one speaker, why doesn't the next speaker leave well enough alone? No matter how well constructed a joke is, experienced speakers usually find ways to improve it from their point of view, to tailor it for their own delivery, their specific speech, or their particular audience. No less an authority than comedienne Phyllis Diller says that learning to edit her own material effectively was a major turning point in her career.

Some joke editing is easy and obvious, such as localizing and personalizing, that is, using local places and names when they fit the gag. When they fit! Most jokes about Philadelphia, for example, don't make sense when told about New York. But effective joke editing goes way beyond mere name dropping.

We can learn a lot about the objectives and the techniques of editing by studying the blue pencil job the economist did on the story of the farmer who lost his pigs in the flood. Let's compare the original and the edited versions of this story, step by step.

The first thing the speaker did was to write a good *lead-in* to make a bridge between his speech and the beginning of the joke.

Original lead-in	*Edited lead-in*
NONE	No matter how much we talk about it, we keep losing sight of the tremendous *human* factor in economics.

You can see how this short paragraph gets the audience thinking in the right direction. It doesn't give away the gag. It doesn't even suggest that a joke is going to be told. But it's a valuable piece of linkage. It helps maintain audience interest, makes the audience want to hear the presumably serious example the speaker is going to cite.

Anyone who can write or outline a good speech ought to be able to invent effective lead-ins.

What was our joke editor's next step? He revised the opening of the joke rather noticeably.

Original opening	*Edited opening*
An elder farmer was moodily regarding the ravages of the flood.	Remember the story of the Arkansas farmer who was wiped out by a flood. Totally dejected, he sadly looked over his soggy and battered acreage.

Again, the changes that were made were not very different from the kinds of changes an experienced public speaker might make in serious or straight material. Clarification and imagery were the main objectives. The phrase "moodily regarding" does not communicate nearly as well as "totally dejected he sadly looked over." The original depends on the phrase "ravages of the flood" to paint an extremely important part of the picture. The economist expanded and dramatized the situation. In doing so he made the joke longer, but better.

Some people have the mistaken impression that editing means taking things "out." Frequently the most effective editing is to put words and ideas "in."

Now let's compare the main part of the joke, including the punchline in the original and edited versions.

Original version	*Edited version*
"Hiram," yelled a neighbor, "Your pigs were all washed down the creek."	"Hiram," a neighbor told him, "Your pigs are all washed down the creek."
"How about Thompson's pigs?" asked the farmer.	"How about Thompson's pigs?" the farmer asked.
"They're gone too."	"They're gone too."
"And Larsen's?"	"And Larsen's?"
"Yes"	"Down the creek."
"Humpf," ejaculated the farmer, cheering up. "Tain't as bad as I thought."	"Humpf," said the farmer. "Tain't as bad as I thought."

No important changes were made until the last line before the punchline. The edited version was greatly strengthened by replacing the single word "yes" with the repetition of the phrase "down the creek."

But the greatest difference is in the payoff. The economist wisely replaced the hopelessly out-of-date and ambiguous verb "ejaculated" with the modern simplicity of "said." Modernization is one of the objectives of the experienced joke editor.

Why should jokes be modernized? Don't old fashioned words and ideas lend a quaint charm to a good old joke? That depends on what parts of the joke we're talking about. The "lost pigs" story actually has *three* characters. The two farmers, and the *speaker.* Notice that the editing did not disturb the quaint, old-time charm of the farmers. "Tain't" was left in. So was "Humpf" and "Hiram." But "ejaculated" was the speaker's word. It's an embarrassingly ambiguous and pompous expression. It needs modernizing to make sure the speaker doesn't come across to the audience as quaint and old-time like the farmers he's poking fun at.

Humor, among other things, is looked on as a very "in" thing. When an audience hears a speaker use corny, old fashioned language to tell a joke, they may get the feeling that he's not the modern, alert, sharp observer of the contemporary scene a humorist is supposed to be. So, no matter how quaint, provincial, historical, or illiterate the characters of a joke are supposed to talk, the narrative parts, the words of the speaker himself, are usually better accepted if they are modern and literate.

The economist made one other important change in the payoff. He took out the phrase "cheering up." Why? Remember our discussion in Chapter 1 about the *revelation?* It's the point where the surprise should explode, and nothing should be allowed to weaken it or tip it off in advance. "Cheering up" starts to reveal the point of the joke prematurely. It runs the risk of tipping off the audience before they get a chance to hear the real laugh line. If the punchline, "Tain't as bad as I thought" is delivered with the necessary *feeling* of "cheering up" no other revelation is needed.

Finally, let's look at one more thing the speaker did to edit the story to his best advantage. He added a very adroit *lead-out* to make absolutely sure the audience understood both the humorous and serious side of the point he was making.

Original lead-out	Edited lead-out
NONE	The fact is, man is willing to endure much hardship if he knows he's not the only one suffering. If he knows he's not the only one whose pigs are down the creek.

This light but serious restatement of the fundamental point of the joke relative to the speech completed the perfect blending of seriousness and humor, which left the audience both amused and persuaded.

With a little imagination and skilled blue penciling the speaker accomplished a number of important editing objectives: lead-in, clarity, modernization, explosive revelation, and lead-out. And, in this case, he did it by *lengthening* instead of shortening the original story.

Make no mistake about it, however, shortening is frequently a necessary objective in good joke editing. Many jokes contain more words and ideas than the speaker wants or needs to make his point and get his laugh.

A clergyman discussing teenage sex problems at a church camp in Pennsylvania says:

> Remember . . . this is the age when a girl's voice changes.
> From "no" to "yes."

It's a skillfully edited short version of the following gag from page 247 of Joey Adams' *Encyclopedia of Humor.*

> Confucious say city she full of teenage girls who have reached the dangerous age when their voices change from "no" to "yes."*

Let's state here and now that there's nothing wrong with Joey Adams' longer version. But the clergyman didn't need the entire joke with all its angles and ideas. He didn't need Confucious. He didn't need "teenage" or "dangerous age," because these two ideas were the main topic of his speech and had been introduced and expanded upon often before the joke was told. The phrase "city she full of" was both unnecessary and trending

---

*From *Encyclopedia of Humor,* copyright © 1968 by Joey Adams, reprinted by permission of the publisher, The Bobbs-Merrill Company, Inc.

toward comedy, plus the fact that it becomes meaningless when you remove Confucious. So, by stripping the original joke of words and ideas that weren't pertinent or necessary, the minister ended up with a much shorter gag that was just as funny and made his point with even greater clarity.

What's the Basic Funny Idea?

After stripping the original joke of all the secondary details . . . the speaker ended up with the BFI—the basic funny idea.

Voice change in girls is from "no" to "yes."

Identifying the BFI is one of the principal secrets of good joke editing. It helps guarantee that the editing will not destroy the humor, that the baby will not be thrown out with the bathwater.

To understand why, let's examine three different versions of a much edited, much told funny story. You've probably heard it several times, and in more than one form.

The first time I ran across it was in this version.

> A timid, conservative, unmarried shopkeeper suddenly came into a small fortune. Overnight, this mild mannered, mincing little man had all the money he could possibly use.
>
> Bravely he snapped his fingers, clicked his heels, and decided to become a swinger.
>
> He bought expensive, mod clothes, had his hair styled, rented a lavish beach villa in Florida, and got a dark, virile tan.
>
> Driving home from the Rolls Royce dealer in his new car, wearing his flashiest sports clothes and swingiest sun glasses, he was suddenly struck dead by a lightning bolt.
>
> Right there in the Florida sun—a fatal lightning bolt.
>
> Up at the Pearly Gates, the shopkeeper angrily faced St. Peter.
>
> "Why would you pick on me like that? I've been a good man all my life. The Lord has always watched over me."
>
> "He was *trying* to watch over you," explained St. Peter. "He just didn't recognize you."

This version was reported by Earl Wilson, as told by singer Perry Como to a New York night club audience.

> A man's wife died and he grieved and grieved until his friends told him he was letting himself go—getting untidy, fat, dull, practically burying himself.
>
> He began dieting, got slim, got a new tailor, got his teeth capped, eventually got a toupee, and met a girl whom he married.
>
> Came the wedding night, the champagne, the low lights—and he dropped dead.
>
> At Heaven's gates he pleaded, "But St. Peter, why did you do this to me, who has always been so loyal, so attentive, so responsive?"
>
> Replied St. Peter, "To tell you the truth, I didn't recognize you."

Here is still another version. This time it was told by a minister to an audience of fellow ministers at a theological conference.

> We must constantly make sure we practice what we preach.
>
> I know of a tragic case where a fellow minister made just one little transgression.
>
> For weeks this preacherly, pious man had admired and coveted a flashy sports coat in a clothing store window.
>
> It was colorful, too colorful for a preacher. For a preacher it was almost blasphemous.
>
> But finally, one afternoon he cracked and went in and bought that blasphemous coat.
>
> It was a bright, sunny day as he stepped out of the clothing store in his gaudy garb. Yet, lo and behold, right there in the bright sunlight he was struck dead by a lightning bolt.
>
> Up in heaven he was dumbfounded as he faced the Lord.
>
> "Lord, O Lord," he said. "Why me? And why so suddenly after all my years of faithful service?"
>
> "Why Reverend Smith," said the Lord. "What a dreadful mistake. We had no idea it was you."

As different as these three versions are, they all clearly have the same BFI. We might state the BFI this way.

> Vanity, greed, or lust causes subject to make changes in appearance. Changed appearance causes God to mistake subject for someone else and to bring about subject's untimely death.

Identification and understanding of a joke's BFI can safely guide a speaker through all kinds of minor and major editing without endangering the humor. With the BFI firmly in mind, for example, a speaker can often change the target from male to female, change the situation from rural to urban, or change the language from illiterate to literate without changing the joke from funny to unfunny.

Three different situations—a Florida spending spree, a second marriage wedding night, and a minister's clothing purchase—are all effective translations of the BFI. And there are many others possible. We could make the situation an aging actress who has her face and bust lifted to help her land young romantic roles, only to be struck down right after a highly successful screen test.

The BFI guides us if we try to shorten the gag.

> Remember the story of the old man who had his face lifted so he could marry a 22 year old girl. His body was 73 years old, but he had a sexy, 25 year old face.
>
> But before the marriage could be consumated he collapsed and died.
>
> Up in Heaven he was frantic. "God, why would you do this to me? Why me?"
>
> "You?" said God. "We didn't know it was *you!*"

Not all speakers, of course, take the trouble to write down the BFI before editing. They don't need to. Their training and instincts lead them to it without the need for an elaborate procedure.

I asked four talented joke editors to work on our #138 about the relationship between fire insurance and cremation.

One revised it from the point of view of insurance companies.

> Insurance companies run into some weird claims these days. Like the woman who had her husband cremated and then tried to collect on her fire insurance.

A second editor also took the insurance company angle but with a facetious, positive approach.

> The insurance business needs new blood, new ideas, and innovative new marketing programs. Like . . . fire insurance for people who plan to be cremated.

A third speaker liked it best as a dumb joke.

> This woman was so dumb . . . she took out a fire insurance policy on her husband because she knew he planned to be cremated.

Our fourth editor produced a great clever gag by simply adding some conflict and a change of motivation.

> Women don't always lose in the battle of the sexes. I know one woman who is really shrewd in her dealings with men.
> She and her husband didn't get along. So . . . before he died . . . just to spite her . . . he cancelled his life insurance.
> But she got even. She had him cremated.
> Then she collected on their fire insurance.

All four worked quickly and skillfully by zeroing in on the BFI, which they knew instinctively can work either forward or backward.

> Fire insurance for cremation.

The major differences from joke to joke took place in the lead-in or early part of the setup.

> Insurance companies run into some weird claims these days.
> The insurance business needs new blood.
> This woman was so dumb . . .
> Women don't always lose in the battle of the sexes.

For the public speaker, the beginning is often the most important part of the joke. That's where he helps his audience step onto the bridge that will take them from the serious to the humorous side. If he doesn't have a good lead-in or opening his audience may not get across.

Not all of the jokes a speaker selects need editing help in the main joke portion. But almost all of them can benefit greatly from some skillful lead-in and bridge building.

Professional comics who do stand-up monologues know the value of bridge building. They call it "blending." They'll jump from subject to subject and target to target with great speed. But they'll blend them together so the audience doesn't get lost.

One of the smoothest bridge-builders among public speakers is a Michigan building materials salesman. Notice how easily but firmly he leads the audience across the bridge in this story that amused a high school athletic banquet.

> I'd like to give special congratulations to you young men who have won college scholarships. You not only cut the mustard on the football field, but in the classroom as well.
>
> It wasn't always like that. There was a time when in many cases neither the athlete nor the college that wanted him gave a hoot about his bookwork.
>
> I remember a particularly lucrative football "ride" that was taken by a star halfback in my town.
>
> During the summer, after graduation, he ran into one of his high school teachers on the street and she asked him what his plans were now that he'd finally struggled out of high school.
>
> "I'm going to college, Ma'am," he said.
>
> "College," she said. "Joe, you never opened a book in four years in high school. What on earth are you going to college for?"
>
> "What am I going to college for?" he said.
>
> "For nine hundred dollars a month and a new Chevy convertible."

Where Should a Joke Begin?

When a really talented speaker humorist is at the rostrum, it's usually impossible to pin-point exactly where a joke begins. Despite this some speakers operate on the erroneous theory that an audience should be advised or warned that a joke is on the way. Incredible as it may seem, one well-known humor encyclopedia actually lists the following as "effective opening lines" for a speaker to use when inserting a joke into a speech.

> Here's one about . . .
>
> Have you heard the joke about . . .
>
> That reminds me of a story . . .
>
> I heard a funny one the other day . . .
>
> Want to hear a good joke?

It's hard to read advice like that without suspecting that your leg is being pulled. Yet it is set forth in this one particular volume with apparent seriousness.

Before leaving the important subject of joke editing, let's look at one other example of how smoothly and strategically humor can be edited into a speech to make it accomplish exactly what the speaker wants it to accomplish.

As President of the Tatham-Laird & Kudner advertising agency, Jerome F. "Jerry" Birn frequently uses humor as an aid in presenting advertising recommendations to client organizations. Recently he appeared before an audience of several hundred woman sales executives to present an advertising idea that had been anticipated for months. He knew that many of the women had some strong personal notions about the general style and form that the new advertising should take.

As an experienced salesman, he knew he needed some kind of humorous and persuasive way of letting his audience know in advance that it would be impossible to meet all of these individual standards with any *one* advertising idea.

His early training as a comedy writer led him to several humorous possibilities. But the best idea, the one he felt most confident about, was a Duffy Daugherty story he had "collected" at a national football awards banquet. The only trouble was, Duffy's joke had an uproarious but raucus punchline, one that was ideal for the mostly male audience at a football dinner, but very possibly too earthy for an audience of sophisticated, stylish business women. He had a great, illustrative joke. His problem was how to shape it and fit it into his speech so that it made his point, got a laugh, but didn't offend anyone.

Mr. Birn's solution was an adroit bit of psychology. He reasoned that if he made his serious point *first*, clearly and unmistakably, his audience would accept his humorous restatement of the theme in good nature.

Here's what he said.

> Now I know that each and every one of you has a firm conviction of exactly what kind of advertising we should run.
>
> For months you've been waiting, thinking to yourselves, "if they'd just ask *my* advice they'd have no problem."

There isn't one of you who wouldn't be willing to stand up here right now and say, "Here's the kind of advertising we should run."

But can you imagine what would happen if we had listened to all that advice?

Can you imagine the chaos and confusion that would have resulted if we had tried sincerely to build an advertising campaign that would have pleased each and every one of you?

Even in Biblical times they knew that too much good advice can produce bad results.

Remember the ancient story of the old, old man in the Holy Land trudging barefoot down a dusty, rocky path?

The rocks were sharp, and they made his feet bleed.

And by his side trudged a small boy with torn sandals. And the sharp rocks cut into his feet too and made them bleed.

And behind them ambled a strong, healthy donkey.

They came to a group of travelers resting beside the road.

"Look at that," said the travelers, "That poor old man with his bleeding feet while that fat, indolent donkey carries no one on his back."

So, the old man shrugged and climbed up on the donkey to continue his journey.

In a mile or so, another group of travelers resting by the roadside looked up and said, "For shame, that grown man riding on the donkey while the poor little boy has his feet cut and bleeding by the sharp stones of the road."

Once again, the old man shrugged and got off the donkey and put the young boy up in his place.

A third group of roadside travelers had still more advice to give. "Look at that fat, healthy donkey with that small boy his only burden. He should carry both the boy and the man."

Again, the old man followed advice and climbed on the donkey behind the boy.

Within a few more miles they came to a rickety bridge over a fast flowing river. And with both man and boy on the donkey's tired back, they started over the bridge.

In the very middle the bridge gave way to the combined weight and man, boy, and donkey plunged into the raging current.

Thanks to their ride, the man and the boy were rested and
managed to swim to shore.

But the tired, weary, over-burdened donkey was drowned.

And it only proves one thing.

If you take advice from everyone ... you'll only end up
losing your ass.

The laughter was deafening—an explosion. But Jerry couldn't
resist the temptation to use the "saver" he had prepared, even
though he didn't need it.

If you object to any of the language in that story, don't
blame me—that's the way they talked in Biblical times.

He got another big laugh. The "saver" proved to be unnecessary because of the strategic and psychological way the joke had
been set up. But, it was funny, so he got two fine laughs from one
great story.

Here we have a case in which the speaker made no important
changes in the original joke that he borrowed from another
speaker. But skillful editing made it fit into his speech, made it
work for him in a situation and context far different from the one
in which it was originally told.

The really successful platform humorists never let their
humor become a parasite. They know how to make it work *for*
them.

5

Three Ways to Turn
Old Jokes into New Jokes

When a speaker uses his editing pencil so radically that the resulting joke is really a brand new piece of humor, he's doing what professional comics and gag writers call "switching."

Switching is a remodeling process, a remodeling process so extensive that often only the foundation remains of the original gag or story. The jokesmith tears apart the original, replaces worn parts, then rebuilds it into a fresh piece of humor that often bears little or no resemblance to the line or yarn that inspired it.

Does such humor deserve to be called new and original? There are a few who criticize it for lack of creativity. "That joke is like a re-capped tire—new tread but same old carcass." And so forth. And, if the switching is transparent and uninspired, and not funny, the criticism is certainly deserved. But when switching is done with imagination and skill, it deserves recognition for what it is, true inventiveness. Any opinions to the contrary can be attributed to either a misunderstanding of the creative process or sour grapes.

The issue becomes especially moot when we consider that, like the perfect crime, the skillful switch is seldom detected. It's generally agreed that the majority of jokes turned out by professionals are switches. We'll never know for sure how many because the funny-for-money men guard their secrets as possessively as professional magicians do their mirrors and trapdoors. But, when done by a professional or skilled amateur, a switch is usually invisible even when the audience is quite familiar with the original joke.

> They say men tend to marry women in the image of their mothers. Not me. My wife is nothing like my mother. My mother always gave me my bottle when I wanted it. My wife keeps hiding it.

That one, from a Baltimore salesman, was inspired by Bishop Sheen's subway story. But if you detected that, you're far more alert and analytical than the average member of the average audience.

What's more, when a switch is funny the audience isn't likely to care about its ancestry. Consider this one from an Atlanta marketing executive.

> Talk about a cheapskate! He's the kind of a guy who gets a hotfoot at a party and then tries to collect on his fire insurance.

The kinship between that and the "cremation" gag isn't apparent until the "revelation" that comes at the very end of the joke. Until the audience hears "fire insurance" there's no hint of the original.

The expert switcher uses all of his creativity and joke construction savvy to disguise his efforts as fully as possible. And, in cases where he can't effect a total disguise, he finds a way to construct the new gag so that the family relationship isn't revealed until the audience is surprised into laughing. Once they're laughing, they seldom question the lineage of the joke.

There is, admittedly, one type of switching in which the whole idea is for the audience to remember the original. Comics and gag writers consider it a mark of professional virtuosity to invent new punchlines for old setups.

> Why did the chicken cross the road? He was afraid to fight.

Or, new setups for old punchlines.

> Why do firemen drink so much beer? To keep their pants up.

But this kind of humor gamesmanship is seldom helpful to the public speaker in his efforts to create useful, illustrative funny material.

For that, the best kind of switching is the complete overhaul, a new joke built on an old foundation. This heavy reconstruction work is not only the easiest and quickest way to produce new humor, it can be an invaluable self-study technique for an aspiring humorist, one of the best ways to learn more about how humor works.

What are these "foundations" on which old jokes are built and upon which new jokes can be constructed? And how does a switcher learn to see underneath a joke and identify its foundation?

There are many different kinds of joke foundations, but most can be grouped into one of three categories for switching purposes.

1. *Connection jokes.*
They depend on an unusual association or connection between two words or ideas.

2. *Formula jokes*
They follow some specific pattern of thought or grammar.

3. *Plot jokes*
Many jokes, like stories and plays, are based on a definite plot.

To help us in our study of switching, we've enlisted the aid of some of the most talented switchers in the peas-and-carrots league. Let's kibbitz as they use these three basic humor categories to turn old jokes into new ones. We'll not only learn more about switching, we'll learn a lot more about how humor actually works.

Learning to Make New Connections

The original "fire insurance" joke in Chapter 4 was based on an unusual but weirdly logical connecting idea: cremation. To switch it our expert looked for a different but equally absurd association or connection: hotfoot. By reducing the original joke to its essential connection he was able to concentrate on the basic funny idea and to find some promising alternatives. In addition to hotfoot, he thought of hotpants and Mexican food. These ideas quickly led to two more switches.

> Talk about a sexy body! I understand that the first time she
> wore hotpants in public ... they had to cancel her fire
> insurance.

> Inflation is affecting everything. Fire insurance rates have
> gone up so high ... lots of people have had to stop eating
> Mexican food.

Notice that all three switches—hotfoot, hotpants and Mexican food—remain "fire insurance" gags. Our switcher tampered with only one end of the original association.

However, if he had done his switching on the other end of the connection, on the insurance rather than on the cremation end, we would have been treated to a series of new cremation gags.

The switch on the Bishop Sheen story, on the other hand, involved both ends.

Subway strap—disciplinary strap

became

Booze bottle—baby bottle

By changing both ends, the switcher pretty well guaranteed that the new joke would be quite different from the old.

But many other effective switches are done without changing either end of the connection. For example, take the women driver gag from the first chapter.

> People say women make lousy drivers. Not so. I've known
> some women who could drive better than men. But I've
> never seen one who could putt.

The strategic connection involves, of course, golf driving versus automobile driving. It requires only a little imaginative reapplication to produce some similar but effective quips, like this one from a New York sales manager.

> Ed says he has to get a new driver's license. What he really
> needs is a new putting license.

The first step in making the new connection method work is to make sure that the switch you intend to make is, indeed, based on a connection. Professionals have various pet names for such humor, "crossovers" and "sidetracks" to name two of the most common. They're good names to keep in mind because they do, in a sense, describe how they work. Look for jokes in which the train of thought is suddenly shunted to another track.

Sometimes they are easy to spot, like William Roylance's neat little one liner we examined earlier.

> You ought to go to work for Maytag . . . as an agitator.

In that one, the connection that causes the derailment is apparent.

> physical agitation—political agitation

Now, the job is to rebuild with different details, with a different idea or situation.

We can retain the "washing machine" angle.

> It's a very conservative little town. About the only agitators
> they have down there are inside washing machines.

Or, we can drop "washing machine" in exchange for some other kind of physical agitation.

> Politically he's a very conservative guy. About the only
> agitating he's ever done is with a pitcher of martinis.

Other connection jokes may be more difficult to recognize, like this one, a favorite of Christian Century magazine editor, Jim Wall.

> In a small town in Georgia, one of the local preachers used
> to go down to the depot every afternoon to watch the 4:14
> go through. He said it was the only thing in town he didn't
> have to push to get started.

A little concentration shows that the essential connection is between these two ideas.

> pushing vehicles—pushing causes

That should quickly suggest lines like these.

> Fund raising drives are like old cars. They don't go until
> someone gives them a push.

> As the old time politician said . . . steering committees are
> fine but not quite as important as pushing committees.

And, of course, hundreds more are possible from the vehicle–cause association. But, see what happens when our switchers restate the connection in even more basic language.

physical pushing–psychological pushing

Now, a little free association thinking turns up a number of examples of each kind of pushing.

physical	*psychological*
doorbells	people
buttons	merchandise
wheelbarrows	ideas
baby buggies	
brooms	
mops	
lawn mowers	

By "crossing over" or interconnecting some of those ideas the panel produces some very different gags.

> How times flies. It seems like only yesterday his father was pushing him in his baby carriage. Now he's pushing his father . . . to buy him a sports car.

> They first met when her car was stalled and he gave her a push. They got married and she's been pushing him ever since.

> Ed says retirement is no great problem for a sales manager. He says it's just a matter of pushing a lawn mower instead of a sales staff.

The extent to which a switched joke resembles the original depends on how completely the original is taken apart, on how bare the bones are scraped.

When the original connection is left intact, vehicles–causes, the switch is apt to be very similar to the original. But when the remodeler translates the original connection into its most fundamental, general terms, physical pushing versus psychological pushing, he opens the door for a wide variety of offshoots which have little or no family resemblance despite their common ancestry.

Switching jokes by the connection method has only one critical limitation, one we've already mentioned. The process must begin with a connection joke. Connections are usually one of two basic types.

1. Two different meanings for the same word, such as two kinds of agitation, pushing, driving, strap, and so on.
2. Unusual associations of two ideas that have only a farfetched relationship, such as fire insurance and cremation, aliens and foreign cars, and so on.

What about the many jokes that aren't based on such connections? For these, other switching procedures are necessary.

Building New Jokes From Old Formulas

Many gags and quips are based on a design or pattern so specific and reliable it deserves to be called a formula. Some of these patterns involve mere word manipulation, others include manipulation of ideas. But once identified and extracted from the original joke, a formula can be used as a foundation for switching. For that matter, once a humor formula has been identified and understood it can be used repeatedly to produce original humor without recourse to switching, and we'll examine that aspect of humor creation more fully in later chapters. For now, we'll discuss formulas as an aid in joke switching.

For their first demonstration, our panel picked one of the wittiest quips by John F. Kennedy.

> Washington D.C. is a city with all the charm of the North
> and all the bustling energy of the South.

Most frequently called the "reverse" formula, it's a matter of converting the best of both worlds into the worst of both worlds. George Bernard Shaw used it when he said, "Suppose the child had *my* body and *your* brains?" It is a very common and very effective humor design.

Our remodeling experts point out first that the Kennedy quip can be switched very slightly and simply from city to person.

> What a personality! He's loaded with Northern charm and
> Southern energy.

With more radical switching, the idea of "city" can be maintained, but we can look for different cities and different characteristics.

> I've always loved Duluth. It's got the warm, sunny climate
> of Quebec and the quaint old world charm of Burbank,
> California.

And, we can stray further, dropping both city and personality.

> The roller derby is a sport with all the glorious pageantry of
> bowling and the sportsmanship of bullfighting.

The reverse is one of the most widely used and most effective of the great humor formulas. It's also among the most switchable.

Another easy to remodel joke pattern is the "semantic" formula.

This is one of Judge Braude's.

> What is called "congestion" in the subway is called "intimacy" in nightclub.*

The humor of the semantic joke should be apparent. Many human activities, qualities and situations are quite similar, but are good or bad depending on circumstances and on the label we have put on them.

To switch it our experts concentrate on some physical activities that are either favorable or unfavorable depending on circumstances.

> In Shea Stadium it's called blocking and tackling. In Central
> Park it's known as mugging.

Take a simple act like scratching one's head. It can be interpreted different ways.

> You may call him an intellectual. I think he's got dandruff.

Another easy to remodel joke formula is the "contradiction" gag. As a point of departure we use one from Leopold Fechtner's *5,000 One and Two Liners for Any and Every Occasion.*

> I never agree with my boss . . . until he says something.†

---

*From the book, *Braude's Treasury of Wit and Humor* by Jacob M. Braude.
© 1964 by Prentice-Hall, Inc. Published by Prentice-Hall, Inc., Englewood Cliffs, New Jersey.

†From the book, *5,000 One and Two Liners for Any and Every Occasion* by Leopold Fechtner. © 1973 by Parker Publishing Company, Inc. Published by Parker Publishing Co., Inc., West Nyack, New York.

It can be switched slightly by finding some different contradictions for the original idea.

> I never agree with my boss ... except during working hours.

Or, it can be switched more extensively by finding different things to contradict as well.

> I never let my wife push me around ... except at home.

> I never take any sass from my mother-in-law ... except when she visits us.

Not all formula jokes are easy to switch. This one, from *Braude's Treasury of Wit and Humor,* follows the "implication" formula.

> The only thing worse than being a bachelor ... is being a bachelor's son.*

There's no mystery about the humor of that one, the trick is to find some other subtle ways to imply the same thing. The switcher must take great care to prevent the original subtlety of the idea from becoming either vague or transparent. Our remodeling crew takes a little more time with this one. Their task is to find other, equally subtle, ways to state the same idea.

> He's a real chip off the old block. He never got married.

> His father and mother were married. But not to each other.

> I think he got married just to prove he could do something the old man couldn't do.

Another joke formula that *is* easy to switch is the "obvious" formula. This one is a familiar classic.

> Someone asked the famous bank robber, Willie Sutton why he robs banks. "Cause," said Willie, "That's where the money is."

The first time I heard it was during a very interesting talk on profitability by a marketing consultant at a publisher's convention in Houston.

---

*From the book, *Braude's Treasury of Wit and Humor* by Jacob M. Braude. ©1964 by Prentice-Hall, Inc. Published by Prentice-Hall, Inc., Englewood Cliffs, New Jersey.

To switch it, the panel first thought of other smart-alec answers Willie might have come up with.

> Because banks have good cash flow
>
> Because the hours are so good

Then, using the same basic formula they produced some similar jokes which depend on either intentional or unintentional misunderstanding of a question.

> My wife asked me why I stop by the tavern every night after work. That's where the booze is.

> I asked him how he manages to get to work an hour late every day. He said, "I'm very punctual."

> After the concert a starry-eyed young lady asked the pianist why he had chosen to play Beethoven's 4th concerto. "Because," he said, "That's what the orchestra was playing."

Whether you call it the "obvious" or "smart-alec" or "misunderstood question" formula, it's fairly easy to spot, and to switch.

Just as connection switching depends on identifying the connection, formula switching requires recognition of the design or pattern upon which the joke is built. How do speakers develop the ability to recognize the formula of a piece of humor? With many it's primarily a matter of becoming fully aware that they exist. Once you become formula-conscious and start looking past the surface of the joke, the lines of the blueprint often are surprisingly apparent.

There is a third category of jokes that are ripe for switching, one that requires still a third switching procedure.

How Joke Switchers Follow Joke Plots

Many jokes have a plot not unlike a story or play. And many speakers have developed the knack of turning these joke plots into new jokes simply by finding a fresh new way to follow the same plot.

The out-with-the-boys gag from Chapter 1 is a good example of a plot joke.

ACT ONE: Couple argues over activity or idea usually thought of as belonging to the male world.

ACT TWO: We assume it is the husband whose actions are being discussed.

ACT THREE: We discover it is the wife who wants to engage in this typically male activity.

You'll notice we have stated this plot in the most basic, factual way. It has none of the interest or humor of the joke itself. Nor does it contain any of the key words or phrases of the original. That's intentional. Just as we found it helpful to translate a connection or a formula in very basic terms, the same principle applies to joke plots. A flat, factual plot translation or outline is of great help to the joke switcher. It forces him to understand the basic idea of the joke and prevents him from becoming too dependent on the original words and specific ideas.

Here are two remodeling jobs our experts produced by following the dull, factual outline for the original out-with-the-boys gag.

My wife and I keep arguing about dirty books. I mean, she's really unreasonable about them. Every night she brings another one home.

My sister and her husband used to fight all the time about stag parties. She finally agreed not to go to them.

Plot jokes are usually based purely on ideas. It is rare when any single word or phrase is vital, such as is the case in most connection jokes. And frequently, a very slight change in the plot outline can spawn a whole new collection of jokes.

For example, if we just reverse the situation in the out-with-the-boys plot, if we make it the *husband* who has typically *female* interests, we find we have the plot for Dick Guy's joke about the wife who goes into the dressing room and is surrounded by sprays and perfumes, which turn out to belong to the husband.

Switching jokes by the plot method is much like what movie and TV writers are so frequently accused of doing. How many times have you heard someone complain "it's the same old plot" after seeing a new film or TV program? Fortunately, jokes are so short and move so fast that the audience seldom stops to make that appraisal. But the television complaint is a good reminder. Speakers who are most successful in building new jokes from old plots take care to bring new situations, new characters, and new ideas to the second-hand plot they are using.

See how slyly one of our speaker-switchers remodeled the "dressing up" gag by giving it a completely different situation.

> I hear that Jim and Nancy Smith had a great time in Europe this summer. It's so great when a couple finally gets a chance to really live it up. They went everywhere and did everything. Paris, Rome, you name it, they saw it and they did it.
>
> But it was so embarrassing coming back home and going through customs. You know how customs officers pry into all your personal belongings.
>
> They opened up a bag and took out three wigs, silk underwear, perfume, hair coloring . . . really embarrassing. And that was just Jim's bag!

How do speakers develop the ability to recognize jokes that have a plot which can be used for remodeling purposes? Simply by concentrating on the jokes and stories they come across and asking themselves key questions. Does anything *happen* in this joke. Is it a joke in which someone does anything? Does the joke deal with a changing situation? And, is that situation in itself aggressive, surprising, or both? Or, is the joke based primarily on a humorous connection, observation, or opinion? Does the humor flow out of the situation, or is the situation just incidental to the humor.

For example, here's a great story from *Braude's Treasury of Wit and Humor.* Is it a plot joke?

> The neighborhood kids had congregated in the front yard when a fire truck zoomed past. Sitting on the front seat was a boxer dog. The children fell to discussing the dog's duties in connection with the fire truck.
>
> "They use him to keep the crowds back when they go to a fire," said a five year old.
>
> "No," said another, "They carry him for good luck."
>
> The third, a boy about six, brought the argument to an abrupt end. "They use the dog," he said firmly, "To find the fire plug."*

  *From the book, *Braude's Treasury of Wit and Humor* by Jacob M. Braude. ©1964 by Prentice-Hall, Inc. Published by Prentice-Hall, Inc., Englewood Cliffs, New Jersey.

As delightful as that story is, and as filled as it is with dialogue, it is not a plot joke. The situation isn't really critical to the humorous idea. The basic funny idea is really a simple connection.

fire dog—fire hydrant

Study this story carefully and make sure you realize why a step by step plot outline will be of little help in switching it.

Now, let's consider another Judge Braude joke that is clearly dependent on a plot, a great one.

> Two moving men were struggling with a big crate in a doorway. They pushed and tugged until they were exhausted, but it wouldn't move.
>
> Finally, the man on the outside said, "We'd better give up, we'll never get it in."
>
> The fellow on the inside said, "What do you mean get it in? I thought you were trying to get it out."

The humor of the story doesn't rest on a word or two or even on a funny connection. It's really a little play, and the plot can be outlined like this.

ACT ONE: Two people try to accomplish something that requires cooperation.

ACT TWO: They fail, but it is assumed that they were cooperating.

ACT THREE: It is discovered they were actually working at cross purposes.

You'll notice, again, that our joke remodelers have stated the plot in very general, uninteresting language.

But, the switch that results is anything but general and uninteresting.

> There was a lot of confusion downtown during the big snow storm. I went over to help a fat lady get into a taxi cab. After pushing and shoving and slipping on the ice I told her I didn't think I could get her in.
>
> She said, "In? I'm trying to get out!"

Most speakers find plot jokes a bit more difficult to switch than connection and formula gags. And, good plot jokes are harder to find and recognize. But once a speaker trains himself to analyze humor for its basic construction, once he learns to identify the blueprint on which the original is built, he begins to realize that these blueprints can be used for a new but similar construction that does deserve to be called original.

All three methods—connection, formula, and plot—work best and produce greater originality when the switcher translates the blueprint into its simplest, most general terms. And that requires the switcher to invent much new material—new characters, new situations, new relationships, and often new insults and new surprises. And that is originality, by any reasonable definition of the word.

6

Solving the Mystery
of Original Humor Creation

If editing and switching can produce a seemingly endless supply of fresh sounding jokes, gags, and stories, why should any speaker go through the ordeal of trying to invent original humor when there's no real need for it? Why try to solve the mystery of original humor creation?

Actually, original humor creation is only a mystery to people who have never had the chance to learn the fundamentals and put them into practice. It's a great challenge. Many speakers who learn to edit and switch fluently just naturally want to move to the next highest plateau, just as model builders like to graduate from "kits" to "scratch-built" after a while. But perhaps the strongest reason for learning to create original humor is that totally original humor offers one great advantage over any other kind. Relevancy. It's almost sure to be more relevant.

Remember the "cross town" gag? It's highly unlikely that editing or switching stock material could have produced that idea. It's hard to imagine finding such a relevant idea in a joke book. The odds against producing a joke like that without the stimulation of the political situation, the governor's personality, and the double meaning of "cross town", are astronomical.

When a speaker works from scratch it's easier for him to tailor his humor to a specific target and a specific audience. When he starts with ideas, events, situations, and personalities that are relevant and topical, the chances are greater that the final gag will be relevant and topical.

Here's another example of how pin-pointedly appropriate original humor can be. A midwest banker had the job of "roasting" a popular professor at a college alumni meeting. The target was a man of great charm and prestige, but he did have a few faults and foibles for a humorist to exploit. One of them was his habitual and frequent use of the expression . . . "I'll buy that" . . . in place of more reasonable affirmatives such as "yes" or "I agree," or even "okay." The roastmaster took that well known cliche, which everyone in the audience had heard too many times, and built this joke.

> One of the things we love most about our guest of honor are his many colorful little pet expressions. But, sometimes they get him into trouble. Sometimes they don't mean exactly what he wants them to mean.
>
> The other day, his wife dragged him to an antique auction. Henry doesn't like antiques, so he kept needling the auctioneer with derogatory asides and loud, unkind stage whispers.
>
> Finally, the auctioneer held up a bedpan of Civil War vintage and, glaring at his front row heckler, said, "I'm sure there are some of you here who won't appreciate the value of this fine old piece."
>
> "I'll buy that," said Henry.
>
> "Ahhhh," cried the auctioneer triumphantly.
>
> "Sold, to the bedpan freak in the front row for seventy-five dollars."

This story owes its origin almost entirely to the inspiration of a specific personality. You don't find "I'll buy that" jokes in joke books. This one had to be built from scratch by an able humorist who knew how to work with the relevant raw material at hand.

The beauty of scratch-built humor is its relevancy. The problem with it, of course, is its difficulty. It's harder to produce—intentionally, that is. Funny ideas occur to almost everyone from time to time. But where are they when we need them?

The difference between a really accomplished original humorist and most of the rest of us is much like the difference between a really fine golfer and the vast army of Sunday swingers. Every once in a while the Sunday swinger makes a really great five-iron shot or cards a birdie. The par golfer simply does it with much greater frequency. The accomplished humorist has much the same advantage over part-time wits, and for most of the same reasons. Most of us play at humor the way we play at golf. We never get serious enough about it to take the time and make the effort to learn how to do it really well.

Thinking Funny is Just Thinking

Earlier I said that speakers who successfully create original humor seem to fall into either the "think funny" school or the "formula" school. As you might expect, the two schools overlap.

You can't make humor formulas work without thinking funny to some extent. And virtually all funny thinkers make frequent, subconscious use of the more common humor formulas. But, there is a difference between the two approaches, not unlike the difference between learning to play the piano by ear and learning to read music. Both types of piano players end up playing the same notes, but their methods of learning what notes to play are quite different.

How does one learn to simply think funny? Well, for openers, as with the play-by-ear piano player, the think funny humorist can learn a lot by the trial and error method, but it's a long process. Fortunately, thinking funny is not as preoccupying as practicing the piano. You don't have to drop everything else in order to do it.

One of New York's best funny thinkers, the marketing director of a major company, points out that thinking funny involves the same brain and the same thought processes as thinking seriously. "I do it all the time," he says. "The two are not contradictory, you don't have to take time out to practice thinking funny."

Most psychologists would agree with him. It's a matter of record that some of the world's greatest ideas have come when the inventor or philosopher was in a playful frame of mind. For all we know, the wheel may have been invented not during some angry effort to move a large rock but during a rollicking, prehistoric log-rolling contest.

So, thinking funny is not only legitimate thinking, it often can produce serious, valuable ideas that might not have occurred if the thinker had been obsessed with the importance of his cerebral mission. But we still haven't really defined what thinking funny is or discovered how it's done.

The easiest way to understand thinking funny is to think of it as the application of a fully developed, continuously alert sense of humor. And everybody knows what a sense of humor is, don't they? Not in the sense we're using the term. Some people use it to describe a "good sport," as a label for someone who can take a joke on himself. We're using it to describe the ability to recognize, generate, and express funny ideas, not as a synonym for "good sport."

My many discussions of the subject with speakers who have fluent and fertile senses of humor indicate one basic truth rather clearly. There is really no such thing as *a* sense of humor. The sense of humor is made up of a number of different "senses" that work together to result in what we call thinking funny.

The Seven Senses of Humor

Just as a successful golf swing is actually made up of a number of vital separate maneuvers, such as stance, grip, arc, hand speed, and wrist cock, a sense of humor is comprised of a number of different and separate senses. And, just as a good golf swing requires that all component maneuvers be executed in harmony, a sense of humor depends on harmonious coordination of its components. That's what makes successful humor as elusive as a successful golf swing. But, just as a golf swing can be improved by practicing the fundamentals, once those fundamentals have been identified and understood, so can a sense of humor. And, unlike a golf swing, humor can be practiced almost any place, with the possible exception of funerals.

It's possible to single out and label a dozen or more senses that play an important role in what's commonly called *a* sense of humor. But in the interest of simplicity we'll concentrate on the seven that seem to be most basic.

1. Sense of irreverence
2. Sense of aggression
3. Sense of fun
4. Sense of discretion
5. Sense of divergence
6. Sense of deception
7. Sense of communication.

Some of these look familiar from the first chapter. They're all important to the telling of jokes. But all seven are even more important to the *creation* of humor.

1. A sense of irreverence

Few of us are so naive and unsophisticated as not to be aware that humanity is amply supplied with vanity, stupidity, greed, dishonesty, and many other defects, plus the hypocrisy to deny their existence. Through his sense of irreverence, the humorist keeps his antennae critically tuned to all of society's defects. He knows instinctively that there's a funny side to almost everything because there's a negative side to almost everything. It gives him his humorous point of view. His sense of irreverence keeps reminding the humorist that nobody's perfect, and keeps him on the lookout for evidence to prove it.

An Atlanta business executive whose sense of irreverence is always finely tuned says he tries to keep it that way by remembering irreverent slogans like these.

> Every silver lining has a cloud.
> There's no such thing as a good boy.
> Two's company, three's against the law.

Irreverence is a powerful tool, even against people and ideas we usually don't hold in reverence. This story is told with great success by a Chicago management consultant.

> I know of one guy who tried in vain to talk his spouse into doing a little wife swapping.

No matter how he argued, she wouldn't hear of it.

Finally, he tried a well known debating tactic.

"*If you were to agree* to swapping, with whom would you like to swap?"

"Well," she said, "I'll tell you. With some guy who wouldn't mind putting up the storm windows."

As you can see, the story irreverently dismisses both the supporters and the opponents of wife swapping. It punches the swingers and the moralists about equally.

With apologies to Dale Carnegie, Dr. Norman Vincent Peale, and others, a humorist's sense of irreverence demonstrates *the power of negative thinking.* It's the sense that keeps the funny thinker constantly aware that there's at least a little greed, a little vanity, a little dishonesty, a little laziness, a little immorality, and a little stupidity in everyone.

2. A sense of aggression

While irreverence drives the humorist to look for the negative, defective, and embarrassing side of things, it is a strong sense of aggression that leads him to turn that irreverence clearly and unmistakably against some person or group. Remember, an audience laughs at people, not at irreverence.

Not all humorists like to acknowledge that aggression is important to humor. They all agree that a joke must be "on" someone, but they feel uncomfortable when words like "aggression" and "insult" are used to describe what they do.

One of the best rostrum wits I know, an executive with a large food company, was surprised to discover how aggressive his humor really was. I had asked him to collect some of his best laughs and to tell me why he thought they went over so well. Here was his interesting comment.

I was surprised to find that about 75 percent of them were "ethnic." Just kidding, of course, but ethnic insults nonetheless. It amazed me because I'm not really that kind of guy."

And he isn't that kind of guy. I've known him for years, and bigotry and intolerance just aren't his style. But he *is* a fine humorist, and his instinct for laughs has led him along a strategically fertile path, even though he hadn't been aware of its direction.

One of the best examples of how important aggression is to successful humor comes from Seymour Kleinman, the New York attorney who gave us the "going public" trade joke, and one of America's outstanding platform humorists.

Mr. Kleinman tells of a favorite story of his that always managed to get a warm chuckle, but never a big laugh.

> A young man decided he wanted to marry a girl just like the girl who married dear old Dad.
>
> So he dated a lot and kept looking for a girl just like his mother.
>
> Finally he met a girl who was a carbon copy. She looked like his mother, talked like her, laughed like her, even frowned like his mother.
>
> He took her home to his folks.
>
> His mother couldn't stand her.

Amusing, but not hilarious.

Finally, after puzzling over it for months, Mr. Kleinman decided to experiment. He made one slight but important change in the punchline.

> His *father* couldn't stand her.

Suddenly the joke was at least twice as funny. It also was at least twice as aggressive. Instead of a mild commentary on the traditional rivalry between protective mother and prospective daughter-in-law, the payoff now revealed volumes about the unhappy state of the parents' marriage, suggesting years of bickering and discord.

A sense of aggression. It's what gives the humorist the instinct to pick a good target and start punching.

3. A sense of fun

Bob Oelrich, the Chicago publisher and toastmaster, believes many speakers fail to get laughs primarily because they have literally forgotten what "fun" is. They've forgotten how to play. They're too tense. Almost all of us had a sense of fun in childhood. As the punchline goes . . . what went wrong? Whatever happened to joking, teasing, razzing, joshing, ribbing, kidding, and poking fun?

The speakers in our survey have a right to be a serious minded lot. They're doctors, lawyers, clergymen, corporation executives, and followers of other occupations that call for serious attitudes. But they all seem to know what fun is. Some of them, like C. Jackson Grayson, one of the nation's leading economists and dean of the SMU business school, will go this far in assessing the importance of just plain "fun" in that elusive mixture we call a sense of humor.

> The psychology of humor is not much more complicated than the psychology of "just kidding" or "poking fun."

Fun not only helps make humor funny, it helps soften the sting of the irreverence and the aggression. And that brings us to the next important component in a sense of humor.

4. A sense of discretion

Of all the principles and theories on which our panel of experts are agreed, the most solid agreement is on this simple but vital rule.

> Humor needs an element of "fair play." The bite of the humor must be tempered, or the audience may resent the attack and not laugh.

At this point humor really becomes elusive. The humorist must be aggressive and discreet at the same time. He must throw a punch that's hard enough to get a laugh but soft enough to be accepted as appropriate for the occasion and the target. This requirement is a little bit like the golfer having to swing hard enough to clear the creek but easy enough to get a straight shot. This little balancing act is probably the most difficult thing for a humorist to learn. Anybody can be discreet without being aggressive, and vice versa. To be both at the same time takes some real finesse.

Fortunately, as we've already discussed, the humorist has some help in his efforts to straddle this fence. A sense of fun helps assure the audience the humorist is just kidding, and the wit and cleverness of the material helps soften the blow.

A druggist used these two quips while roasting a fellow service club member.

> He made an almost perfect score on his I.Q. test: 97.
>
> And I know you'll be glad to hear that he finally sold his luxurious fishing cottage in Wisconsin. To the Army. They're going to use it as an artillery target.

Both were fun and clever, and therefore acceptable.

On the other hand, a business executive friend of mine stepped over the line with this dig.

> Some of our salesmen are just too effeminate. I understand (NAME) has been offered a job as an Avon Lady.

The audience chuckled nervously. It was obvious they thought it was a cheap shot, and its clever wit didn't save it.

As we learned in Chapter 2, there's an easy way to avoid such indiscretions. The speaker could have picked a different target or let the target remain anonymous. For the public speaker specific, identified targets are usually the most effective, but they also represent the greatest risk.

It is a speaker's sense of discretion, of fair play, that tells him instinctively to use easily identified or specifically named targets only when he is sure that the audience will accept the caliber of ammunition he intends to fire. When he is sure, in other words, that the audience accepts his "credentials" as a public executioner for a specific target. That's why certain vulnerable individuals in every group or organization get to be traditional "fall guys." Speakers learn to find out who the safe targets are. They learn to finger the people who, either because of their good nature or their vulnerability, will not have a strong contingent of friends in the audience anxious to rise indignantly to their defense when the humorist pulls the trigger.

A good rule of thumb is this. The less vulnerable the target, the wittier, weaker, and wiser the humor must be.

> As you might expect, our chairman's authoritative influence goes beyond the board room, beyond the corporation. George wears the pants at home too. However, I understand Eleanor decides what kind of pants he buys.

That gentle dig which mixed harmless fun poking with veiled

flattery of both the board chairman and his wife, earned the speaker nothing but warm laughter and affection.

So, at times, a speaker's sense of discretion is more than a matter of fair play. It can be a question of self-preservation. But it requires constant practice to keep it in balance, to keep punching hard enough for a laugh but soft enough to avoid embarrassment, and even catastrophy.

5. A sense of divergence

Much of the clever wit turned out by funny thinkers comes from "divergent thinking." One of the world's experts on the subject, Dr. Edward de Bono of Britain, calls it lateral or sideways thinking. But it could just as accurately be called upside down, backward, or circular thinking. It's the opposite of "convergent" thinking, in which the thinker proceeds logically in a straight line, B follows A, for instance.

The divergent thinker starts out with the notion that A and B may not have anything to do with one another or that A may follow B. He uses "free association" and other seemingly helter-skelter, presumably disorganized thinking techniques to turn up thought clues, unusual connections and angles, and anything else that may lead to logical but unusual solutions and ideas.

Dr. de Bono explains in his remarkable book, *New Think*, that serious, logical, straight-line thinkers are literally dominated, tyranized, by usual and old ideas. They frequently come up with the same ideas others have thought because they keep using the same straight and narrow logical path other thinkers have used and re-used.

To understand how this works, I asked one of the best divergent thinking speakers I know, a Texas newspaper editor, to give us an example of his humorous sideways thinking.

He said, "Okay, consider this problem."

Why would a Jewish girl want to marry a Chinese boy?

"Now," he said, "The serious, logical thinker keeps thinking of such reasonable ideas as: because she loves him, or because she has a great interest in oriental art and philosophy, and so on.

"The divergent thinker looks for unreasonable reasons. He

toys around with all the screwy connections he can turn up between Jewish culture and Chinese culture. He throws all the ideas into the hat, no matter how ridiculous they may seem. Then he tries fitting ideas together, piles ideas on top of ideas, turns ideas upside down and backwards, and finally comes out with unusual but technically logical solutions like these."

> Because she figures he'll do their laundry.
>
> Because she likes the idea of celebrating three New Years.
>
> She likes the way he uses his noodle.

One of the most adroit, most amusing divergent humorists I know is Bob Maitland, cargo advertising director of Pan American World Airways. Bob's humor is not only funny, it's universal. As an executive for a multi-national company, he speaks to Pan Am people from all over the world, and his quips manage to cross over national boundaries with great success.

Here is an example of his sideways thinking from a speech at a Pan Am annual sales meeting in Vienna.

> This is a form we use in the home office. You'll see it's interleaved with carbon paper. We use it to make mistakes in triplicate.

Mr. Maitland's deft divergence led him to an observation that is both unusual and irreverent, but entirely logical. Anything that reproduces correct information will also reproduce incorrect information.

Some divergent ideas are unusual merely because they are obvious. As a matter of fact, one of the oldest joke styles in history is a form of divergent thinking.

> Why did the chicken cross the road? To get to the other side.

And, divergent-obvious humor is as appealing to modern youth as it was to their great grandparents. This kind of gag is very "contemporary" even though it's a kissing cousin to chickens crossing roads and firemen wearing red suspenders.

> I went to a lousy college. As a matter of fact, that was its name . . . Lousy College.

And sometimes divergent thinking can turn up consequences

that are highly literate commentaries on our way of life, such as this classic you probably have heard.

> The modern bathtub was invented in 1856. The telephone was invented in 1870. That means that for 14 years, one could soak peacefully in the bathtub without being called to the telephone.

6. A sense of deception

Many funny ideas, especially those based on divergent thinking, are inherently surprising. Many others are not, and must be made surprising by the manner or context in which they are presented. Putting it another way, an important element in the so-called sense of humor is a sense of "setup" or deception. An awareness that often an audience must be surprised into laughing.

> She uses convenience foods a lot. She has what you might call a Birdseye view of cooking.

That idea has an inherent surprise in it. "Birdseye view" needs only to be explained in the early part of the gag to come as an unexpected pleasure.

> I don't like her cooking.

That idea could be surprising only in some very specific situations and contexts. But, by a sense of deception, a humorist can manipulate the same basic idea and make it surprising.

> Let me tell you what I like about her cooking. Nothing.

Frequently a deceptive build-up consists only of an apparent compliment preceding the punch, like this from an Atlanta food wholesaler.

> Have you all noticed Joe's new tie? Isn't that some tie? It . . . it *is* a tie, isn't it, Joe?

But, even when the basic funny idea does have a built-in surprise it usually can get a better laugh if even more deception is added, as demonstrated in this quip by a Boston public relations man.

> You'll all be happy to hear that my brother-in-law finally found a job. He didn't *get* it, he just *found* it.

The basic idea, finding a job isn't getting a job, is an

unexpected twist. But its laugh power is increased when it is put into an even more surprising train of thought. "Happy to hear" is sheer con-artistry.

Sometimes a very tired idea can be turned into a good laugh by simply pouring more deception into the setup. This comes from a Seattle businessman who was addressing an informal company meeting.

> You'll be glad to know that the auditors have finally come
> up with a workable solution to our cash flow problems. It's
> called . . . bankruptcy.

And, for still another look at this often vital miscommunication, here is an excerpt from a victory speech given by a Connecticut congressman to a mixed group of supporters and opponents.

> I wish I could thank each and every one of you personally
> for helping me win this election. I wish I could thank all of
> you. Obviously, that would be ridiculous, because many of
> you were of no help whatsoever.

A sense of deception tells a speaker that almost any idea can be made surprising if it is preceded by a misleading idea and delivered in a misleading manner.

We've now examined six of the seven senses of humor. Unfortunately, none of the first six is effective unless the seventh is in good working order.

7. A sense of communication

While deception is often vital to humor, clear, non-deceptive communication is even more important. Effective humor requires that both rational and emotional ideas be communicated clearly and quickly, often with poetic precision.

> I would like to make a suggestion that you take my wife.
> Would you please?

Henny Youngman didn't write his famous gag like that, not because his vocabulary lacks depth, but because he knows how extraneous ideas and verbosity can slow down humor and snuff out laughs.

When we think of the redundancies and unnecessary complexities in many business letters and memos, it shouldn't surprise us that some business and professional men simply haven't developed sufficient respect for simple, direct communication to get good laughs.

Successful humorists get to the real meaning with devastating clarity. They don't say "attractive" if they mean "sexy." They don't say "plain" if they mean "ugly." They don't say "of questionable veracity" if they mean "dishonest" or "damn liar." They know that words like "dumb" and "stupid" carry a much stronger emotional wallop than "unintelligent." They know the emotional advantages of a word like "weird" as opposed to "psychotic."

Even when a speaker uses indirect or subtle humor to cater to the sophistication of his audience or to avoid bad taste, there is still a refreshing simplicity and directness within the subtlety.

> He had a medical problem. He was suffering from a severe overdose of Moselbleumchen.

> She was the kind of a divorcee that is best described as a friend of the family man.

Humor depends on quick and clear communication of words and ideas and any unclear expressions. Jumbled word order or scrambled thoughts force the audience to stop, and even back up, in order to figure out what's going on. By that time the laugh pressure has often seeped out of the tank. So, the platform humorists faces all the communication problems the serious speaker faces, but with much greater intensity. When the humorous speaker fails to communicate he pays a much higher price than Mr. Straight does. The humorist not only fails to make his point, he loses his laugh.

Hopefully, our discussion of the seven senses of humor added something to your understanding of what the phrase really means. But to actually sharpen and improve your own, to develop the ability to generate and express original funny ideas in the form of effective gags, quips, jokes, and stories, you need more than understanding. You need practice—effective, productive, meaningful practice. And the easiest, most practical way to practice is to work with humor formulas.

How Do Humor Formulas Work?

Earlier we said humor formulas are much like football plays. They don't guarantee laughs anymore than football plays guarantee long yardage or touchdowns. The results of both depend on how well they are executed. But both are far more productive than chaotic, unsystematic scrambling around.

Humor formulas are *not* familiar joke styles like "Good News-Bad News" or "Confucious say." As interesting as they may be, these stylistic devices are merely ways to express certain funny ideas once they have been created. But the job of creating the funny part isn't made easier by the device. Many people claim they have never heard of such things as humor formulas, have never been conscious of using them. Yet everyone who has ever made up a limerick has used a fertile and still popular humor formula.

Here's another one that works on the rhyming principle.

> Where does a New York basketball player keep his alcoholic beverages?
>
> In a Knickerbocker liquor locker.

Popularily known as "rhymie-stymie," it's a legitimate humor formula. Even school kids know how to make it work. First they pick a noun, and then an adjective that rhymes with it.

> fat rat

That's the payoff. Now, all that's left is to think a moment and invent a question or setup based on a non-rhyming definition of the payoff.

> What do you call an overweight rodent?

Like most kid humor it's too tame and too obvious for adults, but that's not the fault of the formula. Let's do it with adult punch and an adult target.

> What do you call a psychiatrist with an obnoxious personality?
>
> A fink shrink.

And, to further show the power of even a simple humor formula like rhymie-stymie, it can easily be converted from the riddle structure to a straight quip.

> My psychiatrist is really obnoxious. He's kind of a fink
> shrink.

So, for adult use, the formula can be stated like this.

For the payoff, find a derogatory noun-adjective combination that rhymes. For the setup, give a serious and non-rhyming definition of the payoff.

If school kids can do it, so can public speakers.

Why does it work? What makes it funny? An unusual rhyme is a surprising thing. If it is also aggressive, it has an excellent chance of getting a laugh. The phrase "ants in his pants" is pretty well "worn" by now, but originally it was surprising, aggressive, and funny, and its versification played an important role in its humor.

Most humor formulas do not involve rhymes, but many can be learned and operated by thought processes no more difficult than those required for making up simple light verses. The finding of a good pun, for example, requires no more talent or brain power than the search for a good rhyme. The same thing is true for the first humor formula we're going to study right now. It is the most popular of all among public speakers according to our survey, and it is no more difficult to put to work than rhymie-stymie.

The Humor Formula Anybody Can Learn

The "alteration" formula is both self-explanatory and familiar.

> He's the kind of guy who always comes through when the
> chips are up.

Basically, it consists of paraphrasing, irreverent paraphrasing. The speaker simply takes a cliche expression or well-known proverb, epigram, or title of a book, play, film and so on, and alters it aggressively. The alteration itself supplies the surprise element, and the irreverence of the alteration produces the punch.

The noted New York architect Edward Durell Stone is particularly skilled at humorous alterations. He once described his hometown in the South this way.

It's a hotbed of tranquility

A St. Paul, Minnesota broker once introduced the son of a local tycoon with this classic alteration.

I guess we could say he has succeeded in lifting himself by his father's bootstraps.

The district attorney of a midwestern city took a crack at organized crime by altering a modern cliche which is most frequently used in a religious sense.

The juice loan boys actually don't come right out and threaten people who fall behind in their payments.

They call them up and say something inspirational . . . like, today is the *last* day of the rest of your life.

So far, we've looked at simple alterations involving only single word substitutions. Many others are much more elaborate.

A friend of mine who does professional fund raising used this skillful alteration of the title of Dr. Reuben's famous sex book as a title for a speech to some wealthy potential contributors to a fashionable welfare project.

Everything you always wanted to know about charitable tax deductions but were too cheap to ask.

To discourage a major political party from placing his name in nomination for president, General Sherman said, "If nominated I will not run, if elected I will not serve." A corporation vice president came up with this parody alteration.

It's hard to find young people who really want a challenging, responsible position.

After interviewing dozens of them the past few months I get the idea they've adopted the motto: If offered a job I will not accept, if hired I will not work.

The "reverse" is frequently a form of alteration. Certainly John F. Kennedy's description of Washington D.C. was.

An automobile dealer pulled a reverse on one of the oldest cliches in the book to come up with this successful yarn.

To give you an idea of what a calm and imperturbable temperament Larry has, he went to an Italian restaurant the other night and just as the waiter was about to serve he

> tripped and dumped a whole bowl of minestrone right in Larry's lap.
>
> Was Larry angry? Was he even slightly ruffled?
>
> He simply looked up with great dignity and disdain and said, "Waiter . . . I believe there's a soup in my fly."

A Jewish friend of mine came up with this joke by altering one of the best known remarks of the immortal Will Rogers. He told the story to a group organized to foster goodwill among the three major religions in this country. It was a Jewish-Catholic-Protestant crowd pleaser.

> You know, I think there is a better spirit of brotherhood in the country today. I seem to sense it.
>
> Little things seem to say we're making progress.
>
> Like yesterday a Protestant friend of mine said, "You know, I'm just beginning to realize how many of my really good friends . . . you know . . . ah . . . happen to be Jewish.
>
> "There's Manny Goldberg. What a great guy. And Manny Epstein. A beautiful, beautiful human being. And Manny Cohen.
>
> "You know, when I stop to think about it, I never met a Manny I didn't like."

Whether a speaker wants a quick quip or a full-fledged funny story, there's no better starting point than the alteration formula. And it's no more difficult to put to work than the rhymie-stymie. If you doubt it, try it. Remember . . .

> As the great F.D.R. said, we have nothing to fear but . . . failure.

7

How Speakers Get Laughs by Pulling the Rug Out

As easy as the alteration, and in some respects more flexible, are a group of humor formulas we can call rug pull devices. What is a rug pull? That is, what does it mean to a humorist? It's a scheme which permits the speaker to pull the rug out from under his audience psychologically. It's a way to spring a surprising insult with just simple psychological maneuvering.

The rug pull doesn't demand difficult wit or other mental gymnastics. To pull the rug out a speaker doesn't have to rely on clever double meaning. Nor does he have to invent imaginative exaggerations, outlandish analogies, or complicated situations. The rug pull makes only two important demands on a speaker. He must know who his best targets are and the best kind of ammunition to fire at them. Can anything so simple be effective?

Many highly entertaining and amusing speakers manage to produce a virtually unlimited supply of gags, quips, and funny stories without ever getting any more deeply involved in humor technique than the rug pull. I know of some speakers who can use the same rug pull device over and over again in the same speech without the audience realizing they are being fooled into laughing over and over again by the same basic trick. The rug pull *is* as effective as it is simple. Let's find out what it's like in actual practice.

The Rug Pull in Action

In the following example the publisher of one of the nation's leading magazines is speaking to a convention of advertising executives in New York. He's trying to make the point that in the business world, as in other walks of life, virtuous deeds do not always come from virtuous motives. He wants to remind his audience that businessmen sometimes do good things for questionable reasons.

> It reminds me of the story of the man who overhead his wife and her sister discussing his frequent out-of-town business trips.
>
> The sister kept suggesting that the wife should worry about her husband being unchaperoned at those posh resort convention hotels with so many attractive, unattached career women around.
>
> "Me worry?" said the wife. "Why he'd never cheat on me. He's too loyal . . . too decent . . . too old."

To the audience it was one more bit of evidence that the publisher was a natural born humorist. But the publisher knew there was nothing "natural born" about it. It was simply an effective use of a rug pull by an experienced speaker who knew exactly what he was doing and why.

Let's change the scene to a sports banquet in a city in downstate Illinois. The speaker is a popular and witty football coach at one of the state's smaller but athletically successful colleges. The coach is reminiscing about a quarterback who once played for him.

> All he wanted to do was pass, pass, pass, and pass. He had broad shoulders and a narrow mind.

The marketing director of a corporation that spends millions of dollars in television wants to get a laugh at a sales convention at the expense of his advertising agency. Commenting on their choice of an actress for one of his new television commercials, he says:

> She's beautiful. Really beautiful. Probably the most beautiful fat woman I've ever seen.

We're at a retirement party in Chicago. The chairman of the board is being honored and kidded as he prepares to leave the corporation for a life of ease in Florida. The president is explaining why he, and not one of the other officers of the firm, was chosen to deliver the principal speech.

> We considered having Henry make this speech. After all, Henry's been with the company a long time. He knows Ed intimately. But Henry's just too ... too sentimental, too saccharine for such an occasion.

To complete our rug pull round-up, we eavesdrop on a service club luncheon meeting in Los Angeles. The master of ceremonies is trying to get a decision on which of several theatrical productions the club members will attend in a group with their wives. Someone in the audience yells out the name of a controversial stage play in which the actors all perform in the nude. The emcee responds:

> Are you kidding? Why, that's nothing but a dirty, filthy, cheap piece of pornography masquerading as a work of dramatic art. It's degrading! Can we get tickets?

Now, regardless of how different they may seem, these five pieces of humor are all closely related. They're all excellent examples of the rug pull.

Let's study them individually and see if we can figure out what makes them tick.

The Series

The magazine publisher's story about the man who was too old to cheat on his wife was a classic example of the "series" rug pull. It's also known as "itemization" and "the broken set," but it works just as beautifully and devastatingly no matter what you call it. The entire gag revolves around a series of related reasons for a husband not slipping his leash: he's too loyal ... too decent ... too old. What else can we say about it?

The first two items in the series are complimentary, while the third is downright insulting. The wife gives the husband two pats on the back, then a swift kick in the pants. That's the secret of the series. It creates the strong impression that more of the same is coming. When the speaker throws in the insult, the rug comes flying out from under his audience.

The explanation is as simple as one . . . two . . . three. If a speaker steps to the rostrum and starts to count, "one . . . two," it's almost impossible for the audience not to assume that the next word will be three. When the publisher said "too loyal . . . too decent," he was doing the same thing with ideas instead of numbers. It was almost impossible for his audience to avoid a strong expectation that the next item would be too noble, too fine, or something like that.

Notice how the series formula, almost by definition, forces the humorist to put the revelation at the end of the joke where it belongs.

> . . . too loyal . . . too decent . . . too *old.*

So, the series is a *surprise formula.* The publisher could have used any number of different payoffs—too stupid, too chicken, too ugly. Almost any relevant and insulting reason will work. Almost any appropriate insult can be turned into a surprise, automatically, with the series formula.

The series works fine with one and two word items. But it can be even more effective when the items are more complex, providing they have parallel ideas or phrases. Here's a beautiful example of that principle, as used by a Milwaukee service club emcee to roast a popular club member who had the reputation of being an ardent fisherman and an ardent girl watcher.

> As many of you know, he has just returned from another very successful fishing trip up to Northern Wisconsin.
> As usual, he had fantastic luck.
> He got a five-and-a-half-pound bass, a six-pound northern . . . and a 110-pound waitress.

The same design was used, two pats on the back and a kick in the pants. But notice how he used weights to bind the series together more tightly, to make the items relate even more and thus increase the surprise. The same gag with only a bass, a northern, and a waitress without the weights is not nearly as surprising and, therefore, not nearly as funny.

Series items can be even more elaborate, as in this gag from the nimble wit of the sales manager of a large grocery products firm. He was addressing the opening session of a sales meeting being held in a brand new luxury motor hotel. His audience had been up late the night before sampling the recreational facilities and features of the convention site. Now it was nine o'clock the next morning and time to get down to business.

The sales manager wanted to accomplish three things in his opening remarks. He wanted to comment on the splendor of the convention site. He wanted to compliment the people who selected it and made the arrangements. And he wanted to get a laugh. He did all three like this.

> ... and I want to compliment Ed and Joe for picking out such a great spot for this year's meeting.
>
> Isn't this one of the most exciting hotels on the face of the earth?
>
> (APPLAUSE)
>
> There are so many exciting things to see here.
>
> The swimming pool on the roof, the mural in the main lobby, the blonde in the coffee shop ...

Again, there are two pats and a kick. But notice that the series items are lengthy compared with the items in the previous joke—too loyal ... too decent ... too old. There *is* a practical limit to the length of effective series items. If they're too long and unwieldy they may not be recognized as members of a series. Also, when you come to the last item, which is the payoff, it may be too cumbersome to deliver effectively. But other than that, almost any related ideas, simple or complicated, can form a good series rug pull.

How do speakers develop the knack of thinking them up? To begin with, they *believe* in the technique. They know it works. They trust it. They don't waste time wondering what to do. They concentrate on doing it well. The easiest way to do that is simply to make a list.

A Chicago lawyer who is especially fond of the series and wonderfully skilled in its use simply makes a quick list of compliments and insults that apply to his target. Then he studies the list to find the most interesting and most surprising combination.

I watched him work one night at a dinner meeting at which he was going to introduce the guest speaker. The speaker was the son of a prominent industrialist and had just replaced his retiring father as head of the family business.

During the meal the lawyer kept scribbling on a note pad. I caught glimpses of words and phrases—eyes, golf swing, chin, grandmother, and others I couldn't make out. He fussed and fooled with the list for several minutes, crossing out some items, adding others, and penciling down various combinations. Finally, he seemed satisfied, folded his note paper, and settled down to enjoy his dinner. His introduction got off to an uproarious start like this:

> John, we're very delighted to have you on our program tonight. Most of us don't know you very well, but we're well acquainted with other members of your wonderful family.
>
> I'm sure we've all been noticing how much you take after them.
>
> I would say you have your mother's eyes . . . your uncle's chin . . . and, now, your father's factory.

After the program I asked him how he decided on the final form of the gag and what some of his discarded ideas were. He explained that he'd had a hard time choosing between two good payoffs. His discarded alternate went like this:

> I would say you have your mother's eyes . . . your uncle's chin . . . and, unfortunately, your father's golf swing.

And, I'm sure he had at least two other good possibilities among his notes.

What if a speaker finds it easy to make a list of compliments but can't honestly think of any relevant insults? Experienced speakers who know their target and audience well enough to know how far they can go solve that problem by *inventing* an insult. The humorist has one big advantage. He's just kidding. The audience expects him to kid. He has a kidding license which remains in force just as long as he doesn't step over the strategic boundary between good natured razzing and character assassination.

The following got a hearty laugh at a fund raising dinner even though the payoff insult had no basis in fact, and could not have been true by any stretch of the audience's imagination.

> Our speaker tonight has long been an active supporter of many of our city's leading institutions: the United Fund . . . the Boy Scouts . . . the YMCA . . . and Casey's Topless Bar.

The audience accepted the insult because they knew the speaker was just kidding, but they *laughed* because he surprised them so completely.

Notice that unlike any of our previous series examples, this last one had *three* pats before the kick. Is there any reason for that? It's largely a matter of "feel" and "hunch." In most cases, two pats are sufficient to build to an effective surprise. Three pats are seldom necessary but usually workable. More than three are more apt to slow the joke down than to add anything of importance.

What about one pat before the kick? That wouldn't be the series. There are several effective humor formulas that make use of a simple pat-kick design, but they depend on some additional trick to make them work. For the series stick to the one-two-pow or the one-two-three-pow structure. Nine times out of ten they work best.

The Contrast

The football coach who told about the quarterback who wouldn't do anything but pass pulled the rug out from under his audience by an adroit use of contrasting adjectives. Remember? The jist of the gag was:

> He had *broad* shoulders and a *narrow* mind.

What can we learn from this joke? For one thing, it's an example of the pat-kick design we mentioned a moment ago. The insult is certainly obvious. A quarterback's success depends on his being broad minded enough to mix up his plays. The revelation comes at the end where it should. Until the audience hears "mind" it should be anticipating narrow "hips" or "waist."

The real secret of this formula is the amazing power of contrasting pairs of descriptive words to produce a surprise. Almost any pair of words will work when a derogatory idea is attached to the second one.

This is how a successful investment banker twitted a gathering of brokers.

> I get two things from my broker. Good advice . . . and bad results.

I once heard a priest break up an audience of fellow clergymen with this.

> Let's not call him a lying little shrimp. Let's say he's a short man who tells tall stories.

This one comes from the emcee of a boy's basketball awards dinner.

> During dinner I saw many of you craning your necks to get a look at the main speaker.
> He's this guy on my left. The one with the big blue eyes . . . and the big red nose.

One of my all time favorite contrast quips came from a warm and witty veteran scoutmaster speaking to an audience of parents about his love of the scouting movement and the fun of working with young boys.

> . . . and this little fellow was a typical tenderfoot. He had a clean mind . . . and dirty feet.

How do speakers come up with these contrasts so effortlessly? As they do with the series, they trust the device. They know it works to get a laugh if the speaker works to make it work. They know the real trick is to find an appropriate punchy insult and attach it to the second half of the pair. They'll take opposing adjectives, like thin-fat, for example, and work with them playfully for hours.

> He's the kind of guy who has a thin wallet and a fat head.

> He's got a fat wallet and a thin skin.

> Ever notice how you usually get thin arguments from people with fat heads.

> This farmer was a real loser. He had thin cows and a fat wife.

There's another variation of the contrast. It too is a favorite of many successful speaker humorists. Instead of using contrasting words as a starting point, they use the *same* adjective *twice*. Then they build the insulting contrast by using the key word harmlessly the first time and aggressively the second.

> He's got a fat wallet and a fat head.

> She's got a big heart. Unfortunately she's also got a big mouth.

> When you get that far north you usually find frigid weather and frigid women.

In a further variation the speaker doesn't repeat the key word, but makes sure the audience gets the connection.

> He's got a fat wallet and a head to match.

> You know how generous she must be when I tell you her heart is as big as her mouth.

> . . . and the weather up there is really frigid. Same for the women.

So, the contrast rug can be pulled by manipulating descriptive words in either of two simple ways: by pairing contrasting descriptives against each other, or by using the same descriptive word in contrasting ways.

The Qualification

When the marketing director zinged his advertising agency for having chosen "the most beautiful fat woman I've ever seen" for his TV commercial, he was using the qualification rug pull. Qualifications are neither unusual nor funny in much everyday language. I think you'll agree that this kind of thought is expressed so frequently as to be utterly commonplace.

> I think he's an excellent administrator. Excellent. Not too good on imaginative problem solving, but a fine administrator.

But see what happens when we put in a real zinger in place of the gentle, sincere qualification used above.

> I think he's an excellent administrator. Just excellent. When he's sober.

Now we have another pat-kick design, this one based on a compliment that is quickly and aggressively qualified. Most speakers find qualification an easy rug to pull because nearly any statement of approval can be insultingly qualified no matter how lavish and enthusiastic the praise may sound. As a matter of fact, it sometimes seems that the more lavish and enthusiastic the praise, the more surprising and humorous the qualification.

Successful platform humorists are constantly on the lookout for compliments and praise that can be amusingly qualified. They know they can take a presumably sincere slap on the back like this:

> She has beautiful eyes . . . really beautiful eyes.

. . . give it a slapstick qualification:

> Three of them.

. . . or:

> One's green, the other's red.

. . . give it a more sophisticated touch:

> Like a Picasso . . . both on the same side of her nose.

. . . or, make it more subtle:

> Unfortunately, they're a bit too close together.

But qualification is by no means limited to attacks on feminine pulchritude. The following is attributed to a Chevrolet dealer speaking to a regional sales meeting.

> I think the Pinto is a great little automobile. That is, if your family needs a nice fourth car.

And it's switchable too. No sooner had that gag gotten into circulation than a Volkswagen dealer delighted a VW sales meeting with this.

> I think the Pinto and Vega are great cars . . . great cars. For midgets.

Some of the best "qualifiers" in the banquet league make a practice of keeping qualifying words and phrases at tongue tip to make sure they don't miss any opportunities, qualifying language like: but, unfortunately, except for one thing, and so on.

Thus, a politician preparing a speech may come up with a phrase like this:

I'll admit my opponent is a great old boy.

Then, depending on the qualifiers that come to mind, pay the line off in any of several different ways:

Unfortunately he's more old than boy.

. . . or:

If you happen to like old boys.

The secret of the qualification formula is to constantly keep a qualifying frame of mind. And qualifying words and phrases not only help maintain this point of view, they frequently suggest the best possible wording for the final gag.

The Opposite

Why did the company president get such uproarious laughter at the retirement party when he suggested that another company executive was "too sentimental . . . too saccharine" to make the principal speech? Surely you've guessed that the speaker was describing just the opposite of the target's true personality, and that everyone in the audience realized it.

The surprise and insult in the opposite technique come from the simple act of selecting some well-known and somewhat extreme characteristic of the target and then pretending that the exact opposite is true, often with an air of complete innocence. Technically, this is known as "irony." But irony means other things too, so we have a more precise, although more elementary, definition if we call it simply the "opposite" rug pull. It's simple, but surprisingly effective. While mastering ceremonies at a packaging convention, a marketing director pulled all of these opposite gags in one brief but successful keynote speech.

> One of the great things about a convention like this is getting to see so many people you don't see very often. At lunch today a bunch of us were renewing friendships.
>
> Willard was there, giving us his latest hangover remedy.
>
> It was good to see Mildred again. Mildred's just as big a flirt as ever. She was really giving Frank the eye.
>
> And Frank! Frank was monopolizing the conversation, as usual. Can't someone figure out how to get Frank to shut up once in a while?

> It was good to see Joe again. Joe is letting his hair grow.
> Unfortunately it isn't.
>
> And Peter! How great to see Peter again. As usual, Peter
> insisted on picking up the check.

Every line got a good laugh because every claim was the exact opposite of the truth, and the audience was well aware of it. Willard never touches a drop of booze. Mildred is arrow straight and about as far from a flirt as a pretty girl can get. Frank, of course, is Mr. Silence. You've heard of a man of few words? Frank is usually a man of no words. Joe, you've guessed it, is bald. And Peter, although well liked, has an unspoken but widely known reputation for being slow on the draw when the waiter brings the check.

The opposite is an easy rug to pull—maybe the easiest. But it does demand two absolutely essential ingredients.

1. The target must have a reasonably *extreme* trait, extreme enough so that pretending that the opposite is true becomes aggressive. It's even better if the trait is objectionable.

2. This extreme trait must be well known to a clear majority of the audience so that they'll catch on fast when the speaker pretends the opposite is the case.

This means that for the opposite rug pull, the speaker must have a very good fix on both his target and his audience. This is important in all humor, of course, but it is critical for the opposite formula.

The Pompous

The service club master of ceremonies who first attacked the idea of attending a nude stage play and then suddenly capitulated was giving his audience the enjoyable treat of seeing pomposity punctured. We all like to see confirmation and re-confirmation that in every "goodie-goodie" there is a little "bad."

Let's reexamine exactly what the speaker said.

> Are you kidding? Why, that's nothing but a dirty, filthy,
> cheap piece of pornography masquerading as a work of
> dramatic art. It's degrading! Can we get tickets?

The psychology of the gag is pretty obvious. The speaker convincingly and pompously pretended to uphold public morality by the strictest of standards. His sudden turnabout not only caught the audience by surprise, it made mockery of the very lofty virtue he was pretending to uphold.

When executed properly, the pompous rug pull builds real tension. The audience yearns to have the hypocrisy exposed even though they may know full well that the speaker himself is merely role playing.

An executive of a New York management consulting firm uses the pompous rug pull frequently in sales training work. He gets laughs and applause in seminar after seminar with this one.

> Gentlemen, if you think for one minute you can motivate men with money, if you think mere money will inspire a man to work long hours and spend days and even weeks away from home, if you think you can get a man to put in that extra effort that separates the successful from the unsuccessful just by promising him a fatter bankbook, if that's what you think, you're absolutely right!

Not all pompous gags require a complete surrender in the payoff. Sometimes the speaker merely shifts gears and points out the other side of the argument. Here's an example from the same management consultant we just quoted.

> Let's never forget . . . money cannot buy happiness, money cannot buy good health, money cannot buy the love of a beautiful woman.
>
> Of course, money *can* buy . . . a Mercedes-Benz, a trip around the world . . .

In our examples so far, the speaker has played the role of the pompous bore. The formula works just as well when the speaker aims the ammunition at another target.

Here are three neat puncture jobs from a midwest school superintendent who has a great affection for down-to-earth language and thought, plus a great wit.

> So . . . this boy's mother calls me up and says, "Teachers don't understand my son. He has great difficulty with overly-structured, goal-oriented tasks."
>
> I said, "I agree. He's lazy as hell."

> Some people ask why we fired the basketball coach. They say he was very good at character building and personality development.

Only trouble was he couldn't build the boy's characters strong enough to get the ball in the basket. He couldn't even develop their personalities so they could make free throws.

Yesterday, one of our most prudent taxpayers called me and said, "The taxpayers of this school district demand vigorous and unstinting scrutiny of every fiscal factor."

Now, you show me a man who demands unstinting scrutiny of fiscal factors, and I'll show you a tightwad.

In each case, the witty school executive took examples of stuffy, holier-than-thou language and attitudes and turned them into great pompous gags by cleverly translating the pompous language to explain what it really means.

One of the most popular style gags, the definition joke, is often a pompous gag.

The doctor said I was suffering from severe muscular trauma. That's a medical term meaning . . . ouch!

So much for pomposity. Whether it's flowery or stuffy language or hypocritical defense of public or private morals, it's ideal grist for the humorist's mill. The speaker needs only to portray the pomposity in a convincing manner in the setup, then deflate it quickly in the payoff with the frank, down-to-earth truth about human nature.

Other Rugs to Pull

We've considered five rug pull devices. There are others, many others. We could say that *all* humor has some rug pull elements in it. But these five are pure rug pull, unencumbered by difficult wit and other more challenging humor techniques. Our survey of top podium laugh-getters around the country shows that these five are among the most frequently used of all humor devices, undoubtedly because they are both easy to create and easy to deliver. It is rare when a funny speech or a humorous introduction doesn't make use of one or two of these five basic rug pull formulas.

8

How Talking Double
Doubles the Laughs

Experienced speakers know there's a big wide world of laughs waiting for them simply because the English language doesn't always mean exactly what it says. Even the word "English" itself is ambiguous. What does a statement like this mean?

He speaks English like a native.

Tarzan spoke English like a native. Like a very inarticulate native.

Before deciding that this is just verbal hair-splitting, consider this. About 50% of the humor that comes from the nightclub stage, the TV screen, and the speakers rostrum is heavily dependent on the inexactness of the language, on the imprecise meaning of thousands of common words like "native" which permit the most deceptive equivocation.

Whether it's called double talk, double meaning, double entendre, ambiguity, or just plain punning, it's easily the most frequently used humor technique. It's not necessarily the easiest to use, just the most frequently used.

One reason for the great frequency of ambiguity in humor is its great flexibility. It can combine with so many of the popular humor formulas.

A lawyer friend of mine combined double meaning with the series formula to produce this successful little dig.

> He's one of our busiest, hardest working judges. Just last week he handled two cases of assault and battery, three cases of armed robbery, and four cases of Budweiser.

A preacher-punster of considerable skill combined punning and alteration for this sociological quip.

> The way marriages seem to break up these days over the slightest kinds of financial problems . . . you get the idea a lot of couples vow to stay together only "until debts do us part."

Puns and other forms of ambiguity can combine with qualification, exaggeration, and with nearly every other humor formula and technique.

What Does Double Meaning Mean to a Speaker?

How exactly does double meaning help a speaker produce funny ideas? Ambiguity of any kind can almost always lead to a surprising idea. Our old friend "Take my wife" is an ideal example. Because it can mean more than one thing, the humorist can use it to deceive his audience into thinking he means it in one sense, and then suddenly reveal that he meant it in its other, derogatory sense.

The ambiguous word "case" is another example, as we saw just a moment ago. The humorist knows he can mislead his audience easily with a two-faced word like case.

> His law practice isn't doing so well. Most of his cases . . .

The audience has a strong compulsion to expect a serious thought completion like any of these.

> . . . are charity cases.
> . . . are low fee cases, such as wills or real estate contracts.
> . . . never go to trial.

This leaves the audience a sitting duck for a sudden cross-over to the other meaning of the word "case."

> . . . come from the liquor store.

. . . have bottles in them.

. . . are the kind you drink.

So, the humorist knows that virtually any ambiguous word, phrase, or sentence provides him with an easy surprise, and that if he goes one step further and adds some punch . . . he has a good chance at a laugh.

Why Speakers Thank God for the Lowly Pun

Despite its tarnished reputation, the pun is easily the best friend the ambiguity-minded humorist has. It is totally undeserving of its ill repute. If the pun were the "lowest form of wit" why should the two greatest writers in the English language, Shakespeare and James Joyce, have enjoyed reputations as master punsters? Why would the Algonquin Hotel "round table" in New York during the 1920's, possibly the most prolific source of wit and humor the world has ever seen, pride itself on being a virtual pun manufacturing plant? If Algonquin circle stars like Dorothy Parker could achieve immortality partly on the strength of punmanship, why should an ordinary public speaker apologize for a funny idea just because it happens to contain a pun?

The fact is, puns have gotten their bad name from bad punsters and bad puns, from obvious puns, tired puns, distorted puns that require gross enunciation by the punster and great tolerance from the audience, and, above all, from pointless puns, from those jokes that contain *nothing but* the pun and have no irreverence, aggression, or any other commentary on any worthwhile target.

It's doubtful that more than 10% of Henny Youngman's fans ever stop to realize or care that his classic "Take my wife. Please." is a pun gag. And how many of Dorothy Parker's millions of admirers ever cared that punning was technically the foundation for such famous quips as this?

His work is not to be tossed off lightly . . . but thrown out with great force.

Well-turned puns, skillfully integrated into sufficiently irreverent ideas, have always been a high, not a low, form of wit. How do speakers develop the knack of spotting pun opportunities? Part of it is as simple as being pun-conscious, being constantly on the lookout. Pun-conscious speakers are conscious of the several different categories of puns.

The Six Different Kinds of Puns

There are at least half a dozen technically different kinds of puns, and speakers who pun easily and successfully are aware of all six.

Type I puns

These are the "invisible" and "inaudible" puns. Take the word "case" for example. There's no way of telling by looking at it or hearing it whether it means a beer, packing, disease, legal, or some other kind of case.

And remember, not all Type I puns are single word puns. A New York employment counselor came up with this one in a speech dealing with uni-sex job trends.

> Not only can men and women both handle most jobs...they can do it side by side with no sexually oriented conflicts.
>
> The other day I asked a telephone switchboard girl how she liked the idea of the phone company hiring males for that kind of work.
>
> She said it was fine with her...that most of the guys are mighty smooth operators.

Go through any page of a dictionary and notice how many words have two, three, four, or even more meanings and shades of meanings. Every one of them is grist for the punster's mill.

Type II puns

These are the sound alike puns. They don't look alike. They're not spelled alike. But they sound exactly, or so closely, alike that to the ear they're easily mistaken for the same word.

One of my all-time favorites was pulled by a veteran newspaper reporter. He was regaling a service club luncheon audience with some tales of some of the legendary drinkers in the newspaper business.

> Then, there was Paul. He really couldn't handle the stuff. Paul would get so smashed we'd literally have to carry him home.
>
> I know. I was one of his regular Paul bearers.

Type II puns, such as Paul-pall, break-brake, and sex-sects, are nearly as plentiful as Type I puns, and generally just as deceptive and surprising.

Type III puns

While Type II puns are exact sound alikes, these puns are the inexact sound alikes. We might call them distorted sound alikes. And there lies the danger. This is where bad punsters give the profession a bad name.

The problem is that while some Type III puns sound very much alike, some sound only slightly alike, and others sound alike only in the punster's imagination.

> Eskimo Christians Italian no lies.

Does that sound enough like "Ask me no questions I'll tell you no lies" to be acceptable?

Another problem with Type III puns is their tendency to lead some punsters into pointless, verbal comedy.

> An African visitor comes into a clearing and finds Tarzan with a bucket of paint, painting rings around the trunks of trees.
>
> After watching the apeman do this for an hour or so he finally asks, "Tarzan, how long are you going to keep that up?"
>
> "Ugh," said the apeman. "Tarzan stripes forever."

The pun itself is not too distorted. But the joke is about as childish and pointless as any you can find.

A joke like that offers an audience little more than the pun and the temptation to dissect it, inspect it, and, usually, reject it with a groan. Contrast that with the many great pun jokes in which the audience doesn't even realize that the surprise comes from a pun.

> How do porcupines make love? Very carefully.

Speakers who make puns work for them know that the brilliance of the pun is not nearly as important as the brilliance of its application, as the quality of the ammunition and the vulnerability of the target.

Type IV puns

These are what we might call "forced" or "interpreted" puns. The speaker takes perfectly legitimate words, usually foreign words or esoteric English words, and makes them seem to have another meaning. But, the double meaning is really imaginary, implied by the context and by the speaker's inflection, emphasis, and salesmanship.

> While walking to the podium, the violinist slipped and fell and sprained his pizzicato.

Here's a real gem pulled by a foreign news correspondent during a question and answer session following his speech to a business executive's group.

> The question is . . . do I think that the current unrest in France could result in a coup d' etat?
> No, I think it'll be more of a poup poup p' doux.

The fact is that any foreign or pretentious word can be given an imaginary suggestive or silly meaning by treating it as if it *did* have such a meaning.

> I told this girl she had a couple of beautiful tibias. She slapped my face.

> Whatever happened to joie de vivre? He's alive and well and living in Philadelphia.

> He said he thought we should have an ad valorem tax. I said, why not, we have a tax on everything else.

Type IV puns may well be the easiest of all to pull. The speaker needs only to take a word that is not well known and universally understood and pretend that it means something else.

Type V puns

These are related to both the distorted and forced puns, Types III and IV. They might be called "telescoped" puns, because the idea is to take parts of two words and telescope them into one new manufactured word that seems to suggest the meanings of both original words.

A broker used this one while speaking to an investment club.

When that happens to a company it has a financial hernia
and has to go through bankrupture.

Notice that the meaning of "bankrupture" was strengthened by the clever definition—financial hernia.

Type V puns are probably the most difficult to do well. The best are very, very good. But they're few and far between unless a speaker happens to make a hobby of them and adopt them as his specialty.

Type VI puns

This last pun category is in some respects the opposite of Type V. Instead of cramming or telescoping two words together, the speaker takes two words that usually go together and splits them apart, punning on one or both.

My wife is a real back breaker. She keeps backing into the
garage door and breaking it.

Type VI puns, too, are fairly rare except when a speaker is especially fond of them and makes a point of looking for them.

One of my favorites came from the chairman of the board of a small midwest manufacturing company during one of the firm's highly informal shareholder's meetings.

George told me he had a big weekend.

I know his end is big . . . but I didn't realize it was weak.

Professional comics and gag writers use split puns frequently but, like telescoped puns, they're relatively uncommon on the speaker's platform. They're really just double puns, and once a speaker becomes adept at single puns, he may find himself spotting and exploiting double pun opportunities more often.

Learning to Talk Double Fluently

There's more to double talk than punning, and speakers who learn to make the most of the great ambiguity of our language develop a keen awareness for it in all its forms.

No news is good news.

The double and triple meaning of that simple sentence is caused, not by the multiple meanings of any one word, but by the *grammatical* ambiguity of the entire sentence.

> I told my brother-in-law that no news is good news. So he called up *The New York Times* and cancelled his subscription.

Sometimes ambiguity comes from simply a lack of information.

> Here's a juicy item ... Ed and his secretary are going to Florida.

There's nothing grammatically wrong with that. It simply doesn't tell us enough. We still don't know which of two main possibilities applies. Until the payoff, that is.

> She's going in January ... Ed's going in March.

Bad grammar also is good raw material for the humorist. Anyone who's ever read a 6th grade English theme is familiar with the kind of grammatical snafu on which this gag is based.

> There she was, walking down 5th Avenue with her poodle wearing hot pants. Her poodle just doesn't have the legs for hot pants.

Somewhere in between grammatical ambiguity and the pun is the cliche expression, and many a successful platform humorist has built his reputation by making a profession of destroying cliches.

One of the best cliche killers in the peas-and-carrots league is a furniture dealer. Here are samples of his talent in action during the roasting of a fellow service club member.

> I've been asked to stand up here and sing the praises of our guest of dishonor.
>
> I would like to be able to sing Ed's praises. Unfortunately, I can't carry a tune. Certainly not this tune.
>
> And, after reading over the lyrics of what a great guy he's supposed to be, I can't bring myself even to *recite* Ed's praises.
>
> Every successful man finds some route to the top. Some

way to climb the rungs of the corporate ladder. With some it's through sales, with others it's through finance . . . with Ed it was through nepotism.

You know what nepotism is. That's when a young man enjoys the pleasure of his father's company. Or corporation.

Notice how the speaker joined the two cliche gags together with a neat series joke: sales, finance, nepotism. And, of course, his attack on those two great cliches "sing the praises of" and "the pleasure of one's company" produced highly successful insulting surprises.

Reducing cliches to their usually absurd literal meaning is a pretty reliable humor production technique. It's just another of the many different kinds of double talk that a speaker can use to add surprise to insult.

As we look over our survey of highly successful platform humorists, we're not surprised to find the best double talkers among people whose jobs and occupations require great skill with the language—lawyers, educators, clergymen, journalists, advertising people, and so on. One of the main professional concerns lawyers have, for example, is to spot ambiguous language in contracts and other legal documents. It's not surprising that they are skilled in detecting it in non-legal matters and using it humorously on the speaker's platform.

But you don't have to be a lawyer to be an accomplished punster or grammatical double talker. Any reasonably intelligent person can consciously set out to improve his awareness of ambiguity. But that alone doesn't guarantee humor. Ambiguity is very seldom funny by itself. It's really just the surprising foundation on which humor can be built. It's one of the very best deceptive tools on the humorist's workbench. But, most of the time, it is just a tool. The speaker must make something with it. Something punchy.

9

Adding Advanced Humor Techniques to Your Repertoire

Most of the humor formulas we've studied are fairly easy to use. Most of them are quite specific, easily recognized patterns into which ideas and words can be inserted, much as numbers are plugged into mathematical formulas. The series, for example, is almost as reliable as the formula for the circumference of a circle.

The formulas we're going to consider now are not nearly as definite in their construction, and not nearly as automatic in their operation. They're really not formulas at all. They're more accurately labeled humor techniques. And, to make matters even more confusing, they're not exclusively humor techniques. Most of them work equally well as aids in producing quite serious ideas. Exaggeration, for example, occurs frequently in very unfunny speeches. The problem is not one of learning how to exaggerate. Anybody can do that. The problem is one of learning how to make exaggerations funny.

Are these techniques really more advanced, more difficult? Many speakers feel they are. And according to our survey, they show up in original platform humor less frequently than do the easier, plug-in formulas. Most of them require the humorist to "think funny" to a far greater extent than do the set formulas.

If they're that difficult, why bother with them? First, they may not be that difficult for you. Just because our sample of speakers seems to find them harder to execute doesn't mean you will. One or more of them may be right down your psychological alley. Second, added to a humorist's repertoire, they bring a desirable variety to his humor. Third, studying them and practicing them can sharpen one's senses of humor—can improve one's ability to think funny.

Developing Funny Comparisons

Not all comparisons are funny, of course. Most aren't, and some that used to be funny aren't anymore.

Fat as a pig

That probably was funny back in 1587, perhaps even in 1857, but today it's only analogous—with one exception. It probably would be funny under certain circumstances to say that a pig is fat as a pig. But why isn't "fat as a pig" funny anymore except in such an unusual context? It's still aggressive. There's a definite insult there. It just isn't surprising anymore. It ranks along with such tired retreads as "big as a house" and "ugly as a mud fence."

Here's a surprising and funny update of "fat as a pig" from a Tennessee sales manager speaking at a New Orleans sales convention.

> I wanna tell you . . . she was as fat as a pregnant sow with thyroid trouble.

What's the difference between the brand new laugh and the unfunny old cliche? The new line has three surprises—insulting surprises. It uses "sow" instead of "pig," plus the additional obesity of pregnancy and thyroid trouble.

There's another interesting difference. The original was built on the theory that brevity is the soul of wit. The new version proves that frequently complexity, and even verbosity, can be wittier and funnier than brevity.

In the South, where it's almost a patriotic duty to develop a knack for colorful humorous analogies, they know that complex comparisons, the ones with extra dimensions and added angles, are usually funnier than the simple kind.

A New York advertising man who grew up in Texas and, thus, learned the art at an early age, broke up a large client presentation with this one.

> Gentlemen, to get ready for this presentation we've been working harder than a used elephant dealer during a two-for-one sale.

The first idea "harder than a used elephant dealer" is fresh humor by itself. When he added "during a two-for-one sale" he not only added punch, he greatly increased the surprise element.

However, we're not claiming that shorter, simpler comparisons can't be funny. A chamber of commerce official speaking to a labor organization was asked to list some of the good points about an economic system he strongly opposed. His quick analogy was short, simple, and funny.

> That's like asking the Pope how he likes a good Bar Mitzvah.

A Chicago machine tool manufacturer who spent two weeks as a guest counselor at a boy's camp told what it was like in a 13 word description that was worth a thousand pictures.

> You've heard of tennis elbow? Well, meet a guy with ping pong knuckles.

Notice he didn't rely on his audience's ability to automatically think of tennis elbow when he said ping pong knuckles. He made certain they would get the connection by setting it up effectively with "You've heard of tennis elbow?"

Notice too that the ping pong comparison gag does not contain the word "like" or "as" or any other comparison language. Comparison language is not necessary. As a matter of fact, we still have a comparison gag even if the humorist suggests that something *is* something else instead of suggesting it is *like* something else. Technically, or literarily, such a construction becomes a metaphor.

An investment banker speaking to a woman's club in Minneapolis gave this amusing, metaphorical explanation.

> Dun and Bradstreet is what you might call the Duncan Hines of the financial world.

Metaphors are easier to come up with than many speakers realize, and they can make a point quickly and humorously.

He's the George S. Patton of the scouting movement.

She's a bottle of vermouth who's lost her Beefeaters.

Doctor? He's Attila the Hun with a stethoscope.

Many good comparison gags are so stylized that they aren't readily recognized as merely a clever, punchy analogy. For example, here is a favorite joke style of Johnny Carson.

That's my second favorite thing in the whole world. My first favorite thing in the whole world is to go skinny-dipping with the Ty-D-Bol man.

Obviously, Johnny and his writers could have written the line in any of these ways.

That's like going skinny-dipping with the Ty-D-Bol man.

That's about as much fun as going skinny-dipping with the Ty-D-Bol man.

I'd like to do that. And I also am very fond of going skinny-dipping with the Ty-D-Bol man.

The point is, comparison humor can take many different styles and final forms, but it still remains essentially a humorous comparison.

Comparison is so important to humor that one outstanding speaker, Dr. Paul Nadler of Rutgers University, believes nearly all humor is analogous in the final analysis. Dr. Nadler, an economist who is renowned for his ability to speak both seriously and humorously about economics, uses a gag like this, for example, to point out that women can spend money faster than men can earn it.

That's like the motorist getting a tankful of gasoline with the engine running. Finally the attendant says, "Madam, would you mind shutting off the motor? You're gaining on me."

Dr. Nadler uses that gag and many others to draw clear comparisons between humorous situations and serious economic principles and problems.

If you'll check back to the editing work we did on the "football in the chicken yard" gag you'll see that in finding the different points it could make we were really finding different serious situations to which it was analogous. So analogous thinking is an effective humor editing tool.

Here, however, we are considering analogy primarily for its value as a technique for creating humor. It is a helpful place to begin. The final gag may not seem to be a comparison. It may not have words and phrases such as "that's like" or "as" in the final joke. But often, it is a comparison of a serious idea or situation with an irreverent and surprising idea or situation that provides the initial humorous angle or connection.

One of the obvious routes a humorist can take with an analogous beginning is toward exaggeration. A Seattle office supply salesman used analogy to come up with this basic gag.

> I know a guy who went through one of those sex clinics, the kind where the experts watch and tell you what you're doing wrong. He said it was only a little less traumatic than taking your mother-in-law along on your honeymoon.

The story got pretty good laughs, but he decided to further exaggerate the comparison. After trial and error he found he got the best laughs with this.

> It's a lot like spending your honeymoon in Macy's window.

The Secrets of Humorous Exaggeration

If not all exaggerations are funny, what is the difference between exaggerations that get laughs and those that don't? Obviously, funny exaggerations contain a good measure of our two humor basics—insult and surprise, or, if you prefer, cleverness and irreverence.

> It was a bad trip all around. We had miserable accommodations. We stayed in one hotel that was so cheap . . . the Gideon Bibles were paperback.

This successful quip was used by a veteran sales manager in a pep talk to some young sales trainees who were about to embark on their first tour of a genuine sales territory. What made it funny? The exaggeration? Not by itself. Compare it with this cheap hotel story.

> I stayed in a hotel that was so cheap they made me pay for
> my room six years in advance.

That is an outlandish exaggeration. It's also derogatory. But it isn't very clever. See what happens when a similar exaggeration is done cleverly.

> This hotel was so cheap they made me pay in advance ...
> in advance.

If anything, that joke is less of an exaggeration than the "six years" version. But it's a lot cleverer and, therefore, much more humorous.

If there is anything vital that our survey of speakers has to tell us about funny exaggeration it is this: make sure it's clever. It's far better to have a weak exaggeration that's clever than a strong exaggeration that's just exaggerated. It must be irreverent, of course. It must commit aggression against one or more targets. But, above all, it must be clever.

One of my all time favorite exaggerations gags was pulled by a corporation executive at a trade association convention. He'd just been introduced as somewhat of a city-slicker by another speaker who liked to brag about his own "backwoodsy" origin.

> George likes to get your sympathy and turn you against me
> by pointing out that the town he comes from isn't on the
> map.
> Listen ... my whole *county* isn't on the map.

We mentioned that exaggeration plays a key role in many comparison gags. The reverse is also true. Many gags that started out to be exaggerations were improved when the humorist mixed in some analogy.

Notice how similar this joke is to the "ping pong knuckles" comparison of a few pages back.

> I won't say he's in bad shape. But he's the only guy I know
> who can get tennis elbow playing ping pong.

Both gags started by thinking of the possible connections between tennis and ping pong. A little switching on this last one produces another exaggeration gag that is analogous to it.

> Talk about bad shape. He's the only guy I know who can
> throw his back out . . . on the putting green.

The overlapping and interplay between exaggeration and comparison is frequent, dynamic, and sometimes confusing. But each has its own important contribution to make to funny ideas, and to our understanding of humor.

The Humor of Unreasonable Reasoning

The head of an insurance agency in Chicago is known to be a fanatical baseball fan. A fellow executive once introduced him at a sports luncheon with this little dig.

> His idea of a happy Easter is to go out to Sox Park and
> throw colored eggs at the umpire.

It has some elements of comparison and exaggeration in it, but its humor seems to revolve mainly around funny reasoning. It's our old friend divergent thinking. The gag is really an aggressive, divergent "solution" to the following problem.

> How does a fanatical baseball fan celebrate Easter?

It's logical, but absurd—unreasonable reasoning. Switching it with the aid of a pun shows clearly that it *is* unreasonable reasoning and not exaggeration or analogy that makes the gag.

> What does a Catholic baseball fan do on Easter Sunday? He
> goes out and watches the Cardinals play.

Included in the unreasonable reasoning category are funny purposes and funny inventions.

> They've invented a seatbelt especially for backseat drivers.
> It fits over the mouth.

Also included are funny results and funny consequences.

> Some friends of ours got one of those new "picture
> telephones," the kind that give you a TV picture of the
> person at the other end of the line.
>
> I asked him how it was working out. He said, "Very
> interesting."
>
> He said, "I've fallen in love with directory assistance, and
> the other day my wife said, 'Say, that guy who's been
> making those obscene phone calls is kinda cute.'"

Sometimes the humor of unreasonable reasoning gets pretty far-fetched, indeed, like this beauty from Doctor Bornemeier, the former AMA president.

> I know a man who is the product of artificial insemination. Every Father's Day he sends a box of cigars to a syringe in Denver, Colorado.

But, as another Bornemeier story shows, this type of humor can be totally logical and possible. Improbable, perhaps, but possible.

> A man I knew fairly well but hadn't seen for several years called me at two o'clock in the morning and said his wife had a bad stomach ache and that they were sure it was appendicitis.
>
> I said I'd come over but I assured him it couldn't possibly be appendicitis. "Relax," I said in my most soothing bedside-manner voice. "She probably has a touch of indigestion. I took out your wife's appendix ten years ago, and in all of medical history I've never heard of anyone having a second appendix."
>
> "That may be true," he said, "But haven't you ever heard of anybody having a second wife?"

One of the most effective techniques for making unreasonable reasoning funny is to make it contradictory. One of my favorite contradiction quips comes from that thinker of beautiful divergent thoughts, Bob Maitland of Pan Am.

> If I go any faster it'll slow me down.

Another form is the false consolation.

> That reminds me of the guy who came home and found his wife in bed with the milkman and said, "Boy, wait'll I tell the plumber."

Notice that all these funny reasoning gags are simply normal thought processes—solutions, purposes, consequences, and so on—turned into humor by divergent use of the humor basics: insult and surprise.

That's Only the Beginning—Or Is It?

We've now examined 12 humor formulas and techniques in some detail.

There are dozens more. But we'll soon reach the point of diminishing returns if we try to list more. It's far better for a speaker to *master* a few of the easier ones first than to flirt superficially with a larger list.

Mastery of even a few humor formulas and techniques gives a speaker confidence—confidence in himself and confidence in the power of a reliable, workable humor device. After gaining this confidence, a speaker can then proceed to the other formulas that appeal to him most. He can begin breaking down some of his favorite borrowed jokes and extracting the basic formula or blueprint that makes them work. Eventually, formulas and techniques submerge into the subconscious, and the speaker discovers he has managed to develop that most elusive talent, the one many people think you have to be born with, the talent for "thinking funny."

10

How Speakers Turn
Funny Ideas into Funny Stories

Recently, an advertising executive who had worked diligently and successfully with humor formulas posed this problem. He said he was having no difficulty coming up with original funny ideas. Nor was he having trouble putting those ideas into the form of short gags and brief funny remarks. But he was having a great deal of difficulty going beyond the one liner stage. He wanted to be able to create what he called "real jokes." By real jokes he meant what most speakers call the funny story.

His predicament was understandable. A genuine funny story, complete with situation, plot, characters, and even dialogue, is one of the most difficult forms of humor to build from scratch. Because funny stories are longer and usually more complex than short humor, they usually offer more problems to overcome, more pitfalls to avoid.

1. Because a longer setup builds greater audience expectation, the payoff must be especially strong to avoid a letdown.

2. Because a longer setup allows an audience more time to think and anticipate the payoff, more deception may be needed.

3. Because of greater length, there are more places where confusing and extraneous ideas may creep in.

4. Because the main difference between a funny story and a funny gag is the *story* and *not* the *humor,* not one, but two skills are required: humor *and fiction.*

But difficult as funny stories are for many platform humorists, they are relatively easy for others. Just as there are some basic principles and techniques for learning to invent gags and one liners, there are some helpful guidelines for anyone wanting to improve his ability to invent longer, story-like jokes.

Start With a Gag

Most funny stories are expanded gags. The best way to learn to build funny stories is to *start with a gag and expand.* It's not the only way to develop the knack, but it's probably the easiest, and it works.

I asked my ad man friend for an example of an original funny idea that had resisted his effort to turn it into a funny story. His example was a neat little bit of ambiguity built around the popular book and film title, *The Terminal Man.* He saw it this way.

The terminal, man.

Then he disclosed the quip he'd made out of it.

When a customer in a book store asks, "Where's *The Terminal Man?*" he isn't looking for directions to the bus station.

I assured him he was only a few steps away from a good funny story. All he needed to do was to expand the good work he'd already done. He already had a funny idea. He'd chosen a logical setting for the story to take place, the bookstore, and he'd picked two logical characters, the customer and the clerk. A little imaginative expansion would turn it into a longer joke that would fully meet the definition of a funny story.

If the best way to turn a funny idea into a funny story is to start with a gag and expand ... doesn't the funny story building process sound virtually identical to the joke editing procedures we discussed earlier? It does and is, with one big difference. We learned earlier how speakers edit *other people's* jokes. Now we're talking about editing *your own stuff.* That can be a pain in a different side of the neck.

Most of us are able to edit the work of others with a wonderfully dispassionate and objective eye. We can cross out the favorite words and pet expressions of others with professional detachment. But editing *your own* material is uncomfortably like trying to do an honest, objective job of filling out your own youngster's report card. All editing requires genuine creative skill and objectivity, but self-editing requires one thing more, a remarkable harnessing of the ego. For most speakers, that's a problem only up to a point—only up to the point when, sooner or later, they come to full realization of this critical fact.

An audience doesn't care who wrote the joke, only whether or not it's funny.

Once a speaker makes that thought a permanent fixture in his memory, he learns to add, subtract, multiply, and divide his own work with great objectivity. The funny story building process begins with the speaker taking one of his own gag ideas and going through the editing procedure as if it were someone else's idea.

Find a Purpose

This is no time to abandon one of the first principles of effective joke editing, finding a purpose or reason for telling the joke. It's a logical and helpful first step in the expansion process.

My ad man friend didn't take long to find a good excuse for his "terminal man" gag.

> One of the biggest problems facing the retailer today is finding and keeping competent sales clerks. And, many retailers aren't solving the problem.
>
> I know of a book store in town in which if a customer asks, "Where's *The Terminal Man?*" he's likely to be given directions to the bus station.

It's not yet what we'd define as a funny story. It's still a quip or remark rather than a story. But it's on its way. By establishing a purpose or theme for his story, the author has achieved a valuable guideline for further development, just as the author of serious fiction is helped by deciding on a theme or main idea for his story.

Not all gags lend themselves to choice of purpose as readily as the "terminal man" idea.

A Chicago insurance man toyed endlessly with this bit of ambiguity, convinced it would make a strong funny story.

Her late husband's ashes

But he couldn't seem to find a way to advance it any further than this amusing but pointless riddle.

> What is meant by the phrase "her late husband's ashes?"
>
> That's what a woman has left when her husband is late for his morning commuter train and knocks over a loaded ash tray while dashing out of the house.

After weeks of fruitless puzzling he concluded that perhaps he was trying too hard. He decided to take the line of least resistance and pick the most obvious theme or purpose he could think of.

Most ambiguity can be attributed either to wit or lack of wit. He decided to make this an intentionally witty use of double meaning. That led him quickly to hostility. He decided it could be a good example of wifely hostility. He then proceeded to convert his pointless riddle into what, in my opinion, ranks as an illustrative masterpiece.

> Psychologists tell us that many marriages are held together not by love, but by hostility.
>
> I know what they mean. I know one couple whose marriage would fall apart in a few weeks if it weren't for the tender, devoted hostility that binds them together.
>
> It isn't an obvious and violent hostility. There are no vicious tirades, just a continual string of verbal scratches and bites.
>
> For example, the other morning he was in a mad dash to get out of the house, late as usual for his commuter train.
>
> Rushing out of the house he knocked over a loaded ash tray, spilling its contents all over the floor. A real mess.
>
> A few minutes after this unnerving exodus, my wife happened to call on the phone.
>
> "Well," said my wife. "What's new with you, Gladys?"
>
> "Oh, not much," said Gladys. "I'm just getting ready to dispose of my late husband's ashes."

Many speakers find that a helpful chain reaction effect takes place when they begin to build a funny story systematically, starting with a purpose or theme for the basic gag.

When the inventor of this story arbitrarily chose to make the payoff an intentionally witty and hostile remark, he opened the door for his imagination to come up with the highly interesting and amusing commentary on married life that comprises the first half of the finished story. Had he not chosen witty hostility as the central idea for the story, his wonderful opening dissertation might never have occurred to him. His story might have ended up less interesting, less aggressive, and much less amusing.

Make Something Happen

Once a gag has been given a worthwhile purpose in life, it's ready for dramatization. It's ready to have the fiction or story part developed. We could call this procedure plotting. But not all stories have a plot in the popular sense of the word. Even literary experts disagree on the need for a plot. The great playwright John Van Druten said it's only necessary that a play be "about something." Some of the best funny stories are built around what can best be described as a situation, with no real plot, just an exchange of aggressive ideas, for example.

But one thing is certain. For a story to be interesting, something must *happen,* even if what happens contains no more *action* than someone misunderstanding what someone else says, or someone making a witty reply to a provocative remark. And because a story requires that something *happen,* it needs *characters* for that something to *happen to.* And that means these characters and what they do and say must be described by *narration* or *dialogue* or both. And finally, frequently a story needs a *place* to happen, a setting.

There are many other elements in story telling: conflict, motivation, identification, point of view, and so on. Volumes have been written on the art and techniques of fiction. There is little chance for us to condense such a complex subject into a few light pages. We don't really have to. After all, the story-telling speaker doesn't need a novel or a three act play, or even a one act play. Even the longest funny story is seldom longer than the shortest of short stories, and involves only the simple fundamentals of good fiction. All that matters is that we dramatize something aggressive and surprising happening to someone.

The "terminal man" joke creator kept that in mind as he expanded his gag into a story by simply dramatizing what his original quip had already pretty well indicated.

> One of the biggest problems facing the retailer today is finding and keeping competent sales clerks. And many retailers aren't solving the problem.
>
> The other day I was in a downtown book store. The sales clerk came up and asked if he could help me find something.
>
> I said, "Where's *The Terminal Man?*"
>
> "That's easy," said the clerk. "Go out the front door, two blocks south, 'til you see the Greyhound sign."

This piece of humor has now progressed through four of the five stages necessary to produce a successful funny story

1. Basic funny idea

2. Short gag

3. Short gag plus purpose or reason for telling

4. Dramatization

We'll get to the fifth and final stage in a moment. First, let's look at this dramatization stage a little more closely. Notice he made important use of dialogue in his dramatization. He didn't have to. He could have told the story in straight narrative, like this.

> One of the biggest problems facing the retailer is finding and keeping competent sales clerks. And many retailers aren't solving the problem.
>
> The other day I was in a downtown book store and a sales clerk asked if he could help me find something.
>
> I told him I was looking for *The Terminal Man.*
>
> He gave me directions to the Greyhound bus station.

I'm sure we can agree that although the straight narrative version is adequate, it doesn't make the most of the double meaning in the basic idea. The original funny idea, you'll recall, depends on someone misunderstanding a book title for a request for directions in highly contemporary slang. The word "man" obviously becomes an address rather than a noun. I'm sure we can agree that because of that fact alone, dialogue is essential to the best communication of my friend's original idea.

But sometimes dialogue is not only unnecessary, it can result in a much contrived story. The following, a favorite tale of a Houston lawyer, could be told with dialogue, but this straight narration version seems to suit it much better.

> We must remember that it can be a very difficult thing for an individual to curb his criminal tendencies, no matter how sincerely he tries.
>
> I know an embezzler who vowed to go straight. He got an honest job. He fell in love and married a wonderful girl. And they had several years of happiness during which not once did he violate a single local, state, or federal statute.
>
> Finally, his loving wife presented him with a bouncing baby boy.
>
> Unfortunately . . . he presented the doctor with a bouncing check.

This story could have been in the form of a scene of dialogue between the embezzler and a prison warden, for example, in which the warden wonders why on earth the embezzler returned to his old ways after so many years of abstinence. Try it yourself. I think you'll find that it inevitably turns out contrived and unnecessarily long.

As you probably suspect, most accomplished funny story experts, like most successful novelists, find that a *combination* of narration and dialogue is usually the best way to dramatize a story in an interesting and efficient manner. Many successful funny stories follow the pattern of the "minestrone" joke which, you'll recall, is straight narration right up to the memorable line of dialogue that serves as the payoff: "Waiter, I believe there's a soup in my fly."

Dialogue is usually thought to be more vivid, more interesting, and, with no malaprop intended, more dramatic. However, dialogue is also more difficult to invent. That is, good dialogue is more difficult to invent. By good dialogue we mean natural, uncontrived, and believable dialogue, written the way people really talk.

This is not meant to discourage anyone from attempting to liven up funny stories with dialogue, but to encourage them to work to polish and perfect their dialogue so that it does ring true, so that it does sound like real people talk. Reworking and perfecting is the fifth and final stage of the funny story building process.

Polish It Up

One of the oldest but most respected cliches is: good writing isn't written, it's rewritten. It's just as true of most good jokes as it is of any other kind of writing. The theory doesn't have universal approval. No less an expert than Dick Cavett says he usually finds that his original wording of a gag proves to be the best. But Dick Cavett is one of the most talented gag writers in the business, and what is true for him isn't necessarily true for the rest of us. It's probably very much untrue for the average beginner.

In Chapter 4 we learned how experienced platform humorists improve borrowed humor through skillful use of the editing pencil, adding aggressive words and ideas, softening the sting when it threatens to offend rather than amuse, heightening the deception, and, always, clarifying the unclear. The successful original humorist does the same with his own creations.

Here's how the "terminal man" story looked when its author put the final finishing touches to it.

> One of the biggest problems facing the retailer today is finding and keeping competent sales clerks. And, many retailers aren't solving the problem.
>
> You find some real weirdos clerking in retail stores these days.
>
> The other day I was browsing in a downtown book store and a sales clerk came up and said, "Hey, man, can I help you?"
>
> I said, "Yes, I'm looking for *The Terminal Man.*"
>
> "Easy, man," said the clerk. "Go out the front door, two blocks south, 'til you see the Greyhound sign."

Notice how the final version "defines" the clerk as a hippie and in doing so makes him seem more ridiculous and makes his misunderstanding of the phrase "The terminal man" more plausible. Notice, too, that the author inserted the buzz word "weirdo" to further strengthen the level of aggression.

Some masters of the funny story, like Manhattan attorney Seymour Kleinman, carry editing to the level of an art form. Not content with just a flawless funny story that builds to one great laugh at the payoff, they find ways to distribute secondary laughs throughout the setup. It's not uncommon for a real big leaguer to get as many as half a dozen good laughs in the course of a single great story. When that happens, the funny story can easily rival the best comedy of the Broadway stage or television. But a speaker doesn't have to achieve that caliber of performance to take advantage of skillful editing. Even the one-laugh story will usually be funnier if the speaker will only use a sharp blue pencil to improve its clarity, aggression, and deception.

11

Learning to Stick to a Humorous Theme

Even more challenging than the funny story for many speakers is so-called thematic humor, a series of gags, jokes, and stories all dealing with the same target or topic and blended together into a smoothly flowing aggressive dissertation.

The challenge, of course, comes from the fact that the well of ideas runs dry pretty fast when the humorist tries to stay within the narrow confines of a single specific subject. The more specific the subject, the tougher the going. It's hard enough to come up with eight or nine fresh jokes about doctors. But what if the doctors are orthopedic surgeons, or retired orthopedic surgeons, or retired Japanese orthopedic surgeons? The narrower the noose, the tougher the hangman's job.

Why Stick to a Humorous Theme?

If a speaker uses humor only to make specific points now and then, or for the purpose of waking up the audience periodically during his speech, there's no compelling reason for him to string together a series of jokes on the same subject. But there are numerous occasions when it is desirable and even essential for a humorist to keep his material on a narrow gauge track, for example, in introductions. When a speaker is asked to give an amusing introduction to a featured speaker, he's expected to draw his humor from the personality, background, occupation, and other biographical facets of the person he's introducing. The same is true when a speaker takes on a "roasting" assignment. And certainly humor should be somewhat thematic when the audience is highly specialized–for purchasing agents, educators, mechanical engineers, divorcees, for example.

There are many other occasions when one of the principal measures of a speaker's humor will be its thematic excellence. These are tough assignments for the aspiring platform wit. But just as there are helpful techniques for learning to produce individual jokes, there are some good guidelines for acquiring the knack of stringing a series of related jokes together.

Tailoring Humor to a Theme

Perhaps the easiest way to build a string of jokes around a central theme is to make vigorous use of the editing and switching techniques. We know that almost any joke, borrowed or original, can be edited or switched to fit a new target or topic.

This nicely blended volley of gags aimed at a popular New York City physician all seem to be tailored to the target. Yet none of these gags was a "doctor joke" in its original form. The insurance executive who pulled the trigger used editing and switching to come up with every shot.

> We all knew Ed was going to be a big success in medicine when he first opened his practice. He had all the right equipment. X-Ray ... electrocardiograph ... cash register ...
>
> And I think it's especially admirable that Ed has resisted the temptation to become a specialist. He's remained a general practitioner–the kind of a doctor who can do anything ... and charge anything.
>
> But, don't complain about Ed's prices. Ed is one doctor who still believes in house calls. Ed's idea of a house call is ... *you* call ... at *his* house.
>
> You must admit that Ed is an impressive looking physician. He really cuts an impressive figure with his white

> jacket . . . his stethoscope around his neck . . . and his reflecting mirror around his head . . . just beneath his halo.
>
> But to me the best thing about Ed is the way he likes to mix business with pleasure. A few weeks ago he was at a cocktail party and his hostess took the opportunity to ask Ed a few questions about her gall bladder. Two days later she got a bill for $20 for medical consultation. Two days after that, Ed got a bill for $15 for five martinis and 29 hors d'ouevres.

Among accomplished humorous speakers there's probably more editing and switching done for thematic reasons than for any other purpose. But while it's probably the easiest way to get the job done, there are times when more originality is needed to make sure that the target, topic, or subject stays constant through a whole series of gags.

Surrounding a Theme with Humor

Once a speaker has mastered a number of different humor formulas and techniques he develops the ability to literally surround a subject with closely related funny ideas. Systematically he probes every angle of the target or topic, applying his humor skills to every possible opportunity.

Dick Guy, the Waukesha, Wisconsin Rotary wit, is a master of this humor multiplication process. Here's a sample of his thematic prowess from a speech he gave at a testimonial luncheon for a much-loved clergyman who was being transferred to another city.

> I know you all share my pleasure at being here today. As a matter of fact, some of you have told me you've been looking forward to this farewell party for Father _____for several years now.
>
> Speaking on behalf of Rotary, I can truthfully say he has been an esteemed and valued member. Of course, we were a little disappointed by his poor attendance at Ladies Night. However, he had a good excuse. He said all the women would be there in minis and pants suits and he would have felt conspicuous . . . wearing a full skirt.
>
> On the other hand, his enthusiasm for our group singing is absolutely inspirational. Tears fill your eyes at his rendition of "I want a girl."

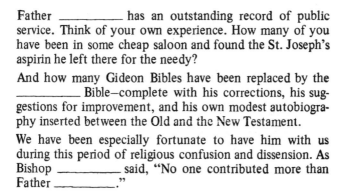

Father _____ has an outstanding record of public service. Think of your own experience. How many of you have been in some cheap saloon and found the St. Joseph's aspirin he left there for the needy?

And how many Gideon Bibles have been replaced by the _____ Bible—complete with his corrections, his suggestions for improvement, and his own modest autobiography inserted between the Old and the New Testament.

We have been especially fortunate to have him with us during this period of religious confusion and dissension. As Bishop _____ said, "No one contributed more than Father _____."

Notice the skillful word play on such seemingly innocent ideas as: look forward to, I want a girl, needy, and St. Joseph's aspirin. Notice, too, the neat grammatical ambiguity he achieved by placing the Bishop's compliment immediately after a negative idea to create an aggressive non sequitur. And, of course, in every gag he again proved his skill with that most sophisticated humor technique—the outrageous untruth.

A performance like this is humor at its most professional level, a half a dozen gags all on the same subject, all blended together in a smoothly flowing, evenly tempered, kindly but aggressive, continually surprising essay. Humor of this caliber is a compliment to both the audience and the guest of honor.

To surround a target like this, the speaker must, consciously or subconsciously, consider every facet of his subject that might conceivably lead to funny ideas. He considers his subject's age, height, weight, sex, appearance, interests, prejudices, virtues, faults, education, occupation, avocations, and even imagined characteristics, and methodically subjects each facet to his irreverent, aggressive, surprising, but fairly tempered sense of humor. Even the most trivial features of the target's personality or the most incidental facts about his lifestyle, experiences, and activities are searched for clues to funny ideas and then subjected to the most divergent combinations and connections.

The modus operandi of both thematic methods we've considered so far has been for the speaker to search over a wide area for funny ideas that fit, or can be made to fit, the theme. There is a third thematic method that seems to work in exactly the opposite way. The humorist finds or invents a central idea that has the power to spawn a whole school of related funny ideas. In this method, everything depends on the fertility of the mother idea.

Working From a Humor Premise

Some ideas, even though they're not particularly amusing by themselves, have the capacity to give birth to a family of funny offspring, providing the humorist serves as obstetrician or midwife.

A tax attorney works nights as a bellhop.

Though not especially amusing as it stands, this premise can lead to a number of amusing consequences.

> He's no help at all with my tax returns, but everytime I get called in by the IRS . . . he carries my briefcase.
>
> His fees aren't too high, but the tips are killing me.
>
> I asked him if he could get me a deduction for my car. He said, "No, but I'll bring you a bucket of ice and some Alka Seltzer."

These three quickies are all related because they all stem from the same basic premise, and there are a lot more where those came from.

Here's another premise. It's simple and zany, but productive.

A timid airline pilot.

The rigorous screening and training given to airline pilots makes this premise ridiculous, of course, but it's plausible . . . well, let's say it's faintly possible. But, once it's accepted in the spirit of humor, it can produce a number of funny ideas when subjected to imaginative, divergent creative thinking.

> I had an unusual flight from Chicago to L.A. The pilot was timid. Really chicken. I knew something was wrong when we passed Davenport, Iowa . . . still taxiing for take-off.
>
> We finally got off the ground, but over Kansas he came on the intercom and warned us that there was a severe thunderstorm just south of Rio de Janeiro.
>
> As we approached Colorado he took one look at the mountains and said, "Folks, would you just as soon fly to Houston this morning?"

> And the Grand Canyon! We got over the Grand Canyon and
> he said, "Folks, this is your Captain speaking. For God's
> sake . . . don't look down!"

Again, all four gags are related to the basic premise and,
therefore, related to each other.

We might liken a humor premise to the premise of a drama.
Like most good dramatic premises, effective humor premises
frequently are based on a conflict, a conflict that promises to end
in victory or defeat. But others are based simply on unusual
situations and relationships which suggest surprising and aggressive
consequences. Many humor premises, such as the two we've
explored, could serve as the basis of a play or a character in a play.
Perhaps the best way to sum up and explain what makes a good
premise is to recall the familiar definition of "news" by a veteran
newspaper editor. He said that when man bites dog, that's news.

As a matter of fact, many good humor premises come from
the daily run of news. A Memphis manufacturer spotted this one
in a local paper.

> An East Tennessee farmer claims his cows are giving more
> milk since IRS agents dumped 40 gallons of illegal corn
> whiskey into his stock pond.

This is not a gag yet, but it is a fertile premise. The Memphis
speaker turned it into a great laugh by following it with an absurd,
aggressive, and surprising consequence.

> That is, they thought it was more milk until they tasted it.
> What the cows were giving was more like Brandy Alexanders.

In this case the speaker was content to draw only one funny
idea out of his premise. Many single gags are developed through
the premise technique. But perhaps the greatest strength of the
premise is its capacity to produce thematic humor, to suggest to
the alert funny thinker groups of related jokes.

To show how prolific and even literate some humor premises
are in the hands of a master, consider this gem from a speech given
before the International Academy of Proctology by former
American Medical Association President, Doctor Walter
Bornemeier.

They say man has succeeded where animals fail because of the clever use of his hands, yet when compared to the hands, the sphincter ani is far superior.

If you place into your cupped hands a mixture of fluid, solid, and gas, and then, through an opening at the bottom, try to let only the gas escape, you will fail. Yet the sphincter ani can do it. The sphincter apparently can differentiate between solid, fluid, and gas.

It apparently can tell whether its owner is alone or with someone, whether standing up or sitting down, whether its owner has his pants on or off.

No other muscle of the body is such a protector of the dignity of man, yet so ready to come to his relief. A muscle like this is worth saving.

The humor of this piece, which clearly rivals Mark Twain at his best, is exceeded only by its powers of communication. It has been reprinted many times in this country and abroad as an example of illustrative writing.

The humor premise is a powerful and prolific device and nearly always keeps the humorist on track, sticking to his theme, because the premise itself establishes the theme. It's not the easiest technique for the beginner, very possibly it is the most difficult. But, as Dr. Bornemeier and many other premise-masters demonstrate, it is a technique worth long hours of study and practice.

12

How Speakers Use Humor to Introduce Other Speakers

Few things are more ingrained in civilized man than the feeling that a speaker must be introduced. The instinct, drive, cultural hunch, or whatever you want to call it is so strong, I suspect, that even when a speaker is a member of the organization he is going to address, even if he has already appeared earlier on the program, there is a conditioned reflex assumption that he must be "introduced" before he makes his official speech.

It's not my purpose to make fun of this introductory instinct. We all have it. But I am suggesting it is probably at the root of the cliche nature of so much introductory oratory. Because so many of us regard introductions as appropriate, that's how they so often turn out, just appropriate.

One of the best ways to lift an introduction above the level of mere perfunctory prattle, of course, is to make it humorous. A funny introduction can accomplish several important things for the introducee and the introducer. And, it can be infinitely more interesting and enjoyable for that important third party involved—the audience.

What's Different About Introductory Humor?

Nothing, of course. Let's remind ourselves once again that humor is humor, and it works the same way in an introduction as it does in the speech itself, or anywhere else, for that matter.

As we've already mentioned, introductory humor is usually more thematic than simple monologue performances. The introducer has a specific job to do above and beyond getting laughs. And, admittedly some humor formulas and techniques seem to lend themselves especially well to introductions. The series, for example, might be called the "introducer's specialty," because its very structure, the listing or itemizing of a series of ideas prior to pulling the rug, permits a speaker to use relevant background information and biographical data as an integral part of the humor.

> Our speaker tonight has the well-deserved reputation of being one of our industry's most inspiring sales managers . . . one of its shrewdest marketing strategists . . . and one of its worst gin rummy players.

This excerpt from an introduction by a Cleveland corporate executive clearly shows the great efficiency of the rug pull in introductory humor. He not only got his laugh, he established the speaker's principal credentials in the process.

As we pointed out in our earlier discussion of the series technique, the series can be used repeatedly without losing surprise power, as the Cleveland speaker demonstrated.

> As a sales manager he knows how to make his salesmen do what he wants and like it. As a marketing strategist he knows how to make the consumer do what he wants and like it. Somehow all this power escapes him when he sits down to play cards.

And, he wasn't through yet.

> He's not only a man of many accomplishments, he's a man of many blessings. He has undoubtedly the most beautiful wife . . . two of the handsomest children . . . and one of the ugliest dogs I've ever seen.

But the series is by no means the only appropriate humor technique for introductions. The contrast, the qualification, the exaggeration, all of them serve the introducer as well as the featured speaker, roastmaster, emcee, or comic. You may have noticed how many of the humor examples we've covered so far have obviously been excerpted from introductions.

What Good Is a Funny Introduction?

Other than the fact that most members of the audience would rather laugh than yawn, what advantages does a humorous introduction have over a straight one?

Assuming that either kind of introduction contains the essential information, biographical highlights, accomplishments, resume, and so on, an amusing introduction can have two important advantages over the serious variety.

1. It can do a better job of selling the speaker to the audience. Many a featured speaker who has no real charisma or wit has been made to appear charming and witty by a charming and witty introduction.

2. It can do a better job of selling the speech itself to the audience. Some topics sound duller than they really are. A talented introductory speaker who can capture the jist of a technically or philsophically complex subject and give it a light and interesting interpretation can greatly improve the chances that the audience will at least make an effort to understand and appreciate the speech to follow.

We might add the obvious point that a humorous introduction also does a better job of selling the introducer to the audience. Many a successful and sought-after speaker first gained his reputation as a rostrum performer, not by making speeches, but by giving witty and amusing introductions to other speakers.

There are exceptions, of course, but generally nearly any introduction will be improved with a little humor no matter how serious the speech is that follows it.

How Humor Can Sell a Speaker to an Audience

Used strategically, humor can create three favorable impressions in an audience about the speaker being introduced.

1. It can paint the speaker as a warm, human personality, someone the audience will accept as a regular, down-to-earth guy or gal.

2. It can create the impression the speaker is clever and witty, giving the audience respect for his or her intellectual capacity.

3. It can encourage an audience to accept the speaker as "one of us," a kindred soul who shares their opinions and prejudices.

The impression produced is largely a matter of targeting. If the introducer uses the speaker as the target of some warmly human digs the audience will tend to develop affection for the target even as it laughs at him. Notice we said "warmly human digs." This is no time for derisive ammunition. The object here is to portray the speaker as likeable and with universal, human foibles, not to picture him as a stupid jerk. When the Cleveland executive poked fun at the sales manager's card sense and his taste in canine pulchritude, he never came close to character assassination. I'll discuss this strategic element in humor in further detail in the next chapter.

What about the two other products of a humorous introduction? If the introducer chooses a target other than the speaker, a target the audience is especially anxious to laugh at, and then puts the upcoming speaker in the role of the marksman who originally fired the ammunition, the audience will get the impression that the speaker himself is witty and that he shares their view of the world as evidenced by their mutual opinion of the third-party target.

Compare the targeting and thrust of this introductory gag with our earlier example.

> Our speaker tonight has many talents, not the least of which is his ability to recognize talent in other people.
>
> I asked him what he thought of Harry's presentation at yesterday's session.
>
> "Not bad," said Joe. "Harry would have a great act if he could just team up with a good ventriloquist."

Here, it is the speaker to follow, not the introducer, who is given credit for firing strong ammunition at a vulnerable third party. The target, Harry, was a popular fall guy. The humor not only made the speaker, Joe, look clever, it put him squarely on the audience's side in their good-natured disapproval of the target. The introducer merely directed the fire.

How Humor Can Sell a Speaker's Speech
to an Audience

A bit more difficult, but just as desirable, is the use of introductory humor to sell the audience on the merits of the speech the speaker is going to deliver. A skillful introducer can heighten the audience's desire to hear what the speaker has to say by building some humor around the topic of the speech itself. See if these lighthearted quips don't whet your appetite for the speech that followed.

> The problems of managing an advertising agency may seem tame compared with the problems of managing a multi-national electronics conglomerate or a major aero-space supplier.
>
> But don't be too sure.
>
> I know one advertising agency executive who was terribly chagrined when a British zoologist came out with a book entitled *The Human Zoo.* "That," said my advertising friend, "was the perfect title for my memoirs."
>
> It's been pointed out many times that an ad agency has no large sums of money tied up in equipment and merchandise, that the management of an ad agency is easy because its entire inventory walks out the door every night at five o'clock.
>
> To which an agency executive friend of mine replied, "Yes, but the trouble is about half of that inventory may not walk back in the door the next morning until 10:30."
>
> I think we have much to learn about management from our speaker this morning. He has faced and solved many management problems that have stumped you and me for years.

That introduction-to-an-introduction given at a management seminar by a Boston management consultant demonstrates, among other things, the strategic directional controls the introductory humorist has, if he will just put those controls to work.

By taking two mild but interesting little jabs at the problems of managing an advertising agency, this introduction served to sell the upcoming speech much as interesting cover blurbs can help sell the contents of a book.

Using Humor to Overcome a Bad Introduction

Occasionally, not often but occasionally, an introduction is so bad the speaker feels compelled to respond to it before beginning his planned talk.

Most often, bad introductions are too complimentary. Some introducers seem to feel the truth isn't good enough for a particularly admirable speaker, so they stretch and pull the truth to the point where it is embarrassing to anyone but a totally ego-centered personality. If the excesses are preposterous to the point of being dishonest, a speaker should offer some tactful corrections to set the record straight. The best way to respond to the occasional saccharin excesses of eulogistic exaggerations is with humor.

Mike Howlett, Illinois Democratic leader and one of the party's most eloquent speakers, has a special dislike for those embarrassing introductory lily gildings. Here is one of Mr. Howlett's favorite responses to that kind of an introduction.

> That's the finest introduction I ever had except one. And that's when I addressed an American Legion convention down in Carbondale and the chairman didn't show up . . . so I introduced myself.

Mike's introduction deflater never misses and is similar to one used by a Madison, Wisconsin lawyer.

> Before I begin I'd like to make two things clear. The speech I'm about to make, I wrote myself. That introduction was written by my mother.

One of the most successful and most surprising jobs of erasing the stigma of an excessively flattering introduction came from a Congregational minister who, after listening to himself virtually deified by a sincere but somewhat immature introductory speaker, came up with this.

> After listening to that introduction I'm a little confused.
>
> Are we going to hear a minister talk about Jesus Christ . . . or Jesus Christ talk about a minister?

Fortunately, introductory excesses and distortions are relatively rare, and it isn't often that a speaker has to reach into his joke file for counter-measures. When it happens, however, a speaker can cut short the embarrassment and win a lot of friends by fighting "put ups" with put-downs.

13

Three Ways to Win Over an Audience with Humor

Just as the introductory speaker has the opportunity to shape and direct his humor to the advantage of the speaker he is presenting, the speechmaker himself has it within his power to use humor tactically and strategically to sell himself to his audience. By flashing his wit he can earn their respect. By attacking their enemies he can gain their loyalty. By sharing their shortcomings and troubles, by playing, in a sense, a fellow clown in the comedy of life, he can win their affection. Again, it's largely a matter of selecting the right targets and firing the right ammunition. But it's not just a piece of cake, as they say. Without the skill and judgment that comes from experience, the wit can become an insufferable bore. The ally can become a mercenary, and the loveable underdog, a fool.

The Humorist as Intellectual

Chicago advertising man Martin A. Cohen has a well-deserved reputation for being bright. Part of it comes from the many bright and effective advertising ideas he comes up with, but some of his reputation is due to the witty remarks he drops into conversations, presentations, and meetings. For example:

> All gall is divided into two parts. Mitigated and unmiti-
> gated.

Quips like that not only shed favorable light on the speaker's intelligence, they're apt to be remembered long after most comic one liners are forgotten.

For most people, clever wit is irrefutable evidence of brains. Even if a line doesn't get a big laugh, if it's intellectually witty it can create the impression that the speaker has great intellectual ability.

Witty thoughts occur to most people who have the intellectual capacity to address important audiences on significant subjects. But too many speakers make the mistake of discarding such intellectual humor because they don't think it will draw big laughs. It's a shame to waste it because of an erroneous impression that laughs have to be audible to be advantageous.

Brainy humor not only enhances the speaker's reputation, as Seymour Kleinman points out, it compliments the audience. It not only assures them that the speaker has intellectual capacity, it lets them know that he realizes they do too, and they are understandably flattered. But the brainier the humor is, the more important it is to try Mr. Kleinman's "I.Q. test" to make sure you're not talking over their heads.

Not all successful intellectual humor is at the Ph.D. level, however. A Cincinnati lawyer made one little switch in a common concept of law and came up with this.

> When I see the size of some of the alimony payments
> being awarded these days . . . I'm expecting some client to
> ask me to get his divorce annulled.

A speaker seldom brings the house down with quips like that. But if the audience understands them, it enjoys them, and the speaker's intelligence goes up a few points in their estimation. This low key, egghead humor should never be forced. That's true of most humor, of course, but it's especially important to be casual and "dry" when delivering amusing material that is more witty than funny.

The Humorist as Hero

If the platform humorist can come off as a brain, he can also be acclaimed as a hero, as a hero who does battle with the common enemies and villains. Critically important, of course, is predetermination of just who are the real enemies and villains in the minds of the audience. To be a hero the speaker picks especially vulnerable targets, people either living or dead, near or far, general or specific, against whom the audience has stored up more than a little hostility—civilized hostility, of course, but hostility nonetheless. Then, the speaker attacks those targets with gladiatorial zeal.

> Ordinarily I would say he has the brains of a chicken . . .
> except that would be a very insulting thing to say . . .
> about a chicken.

That's the kind of straight-arm, red-dog humor that brings protests of "too aggressive" from many people. That is, they find it too aggressive right up until the time they suddenly hear it directed at some person or group they don't like a whole lot. Then, suddenly, it's hilarious. It all depends, as they say, on whose ox is being gored. That type of joke requires careful fitting of strong ammunition to vulnerable targets.

We're not recommending such tactics, but no book on humor would be complete without some acknowledgment of humor as a weapon. Many a successful speaker has been lionized by an audience after conquering an infamous enemy with lethal jokes.

The Humorist as Clown

If there's anything an audience enjoys more than respecting a brain or worshipping a hero, it's sympathizing with an underdog, especially if that underdog shares their defects and vicissitudes, permitting them to see themselves in his place. By playing the role of a clown, a clever platform humorist can manipulate this psychological force to his own benefit. He can actually build strong feelings of affection in his audience.

When we say playing the clown we don't mean using baggy pants and pratfalls, we mean using adroitly self-targeted humor that convinces the audience that the speaker, just like any of them, is, after all, an ordinary human being with the same human limitations, problems, and hangups. Many of the great comedians—

Chaplin, Keaton, Red Skelton, and others—have accomplished this with their theatrical genius. But a speaker with sound humor technique can achieve much the same kind of response without crossing over into the difficult, treacherous field of comedy. He can do it simply by making himself the butt of some lighthearted, but human quips and gags. And, the more prestigious and dignified the speaker, the more effective his artful, self-deprecating clowning can be.

> Here in the business world I'm the Chairman of the Board.
> At home I'm chairman of the storm windows.
>
> My mother-in-law calls me son . . . for short.

Those quips from the repertoires of very important and highly respected businessmen never fail to win friends.

Most successful rostrum wits know how to pull off this respectable clowning in an easy, offhand, convincing manner. Notice we said convincing. Any speaker who, deep down in his heart, is a pompous ass, will find it hard to make an audience believe otherwise just by clowning. Self-targeted humor can be both an effective tool for manipulating audience affection, and for improving one's self perspective.

The Myth of Dignity

Why don't more speakers appreciate and exploit the ingratiating power of such gentle, lighthearted, make-believe self-destruction? Many probably have a misconception of what it means to be dignified. And, admittedly, clowning can be carried too far, past the point of believability to the point of cornball absurdity that can indeed be undignified. But most of us are far more apt to be boring than boorish, much more likely to be stuffy than slapstick, and in much greater danger of being self-important than self-deprecating. Human dignity does not depend on egocentricity. When we speak of the "dignity of man" we don't imply pomposity. If anything, the phrase has the opposite meaning.

One of the finest speakers among Midwest politicians uses self put-downs like this with great success. To my knowledge, no one in either party has ever considered him undignified.

Years ago when I was elected a vice president of my company I came home and proudly told my wife.

She was busy with the kids and she had just finished cooking, and she said, "Vice president ... for heaven's sake! That's a big deal. A big, big deal. Where I buy groceries they even have a vice president in charge of prunes."

So, I questioned that. I said, "Listen, you can't put me on like that. I'm going to find out about this."

So, I called up the supermarket and I said, "Listen, I'd like to speak to the vice president in charge of prunes."

And the girl at the other end of the line said, "Packaged or bulk?"

14

How to Get Serious with Humor

If we've stressed and restressed any point so far, it is the point that the best platform humor makes a point. We've seen that the great majority of accomplished podium wits favor illustrative humor. We've also seen that audiences seem to favor it too. We've speculated that the audience lowers its laugh resistance when the gag or story carries a serious idea or message in addition to the laugh.

But there are additional, more specific reasons why illustrative humor works better than the pointless variety on the speaker's platform. There are at least three serious and functional benefits to be gained from humor that makes a point.

1. Humor can make a speaker's ideas and assertions more *memorable.*

2. Humor can *clarify* what a speaker has to say. Make his ideas easier to understand.

3. Humor can help *persuade.* It can help convince an audience that what a speaker says is right.

Before we examine these claims in more detail, let's make sure we agree on the meaning of the word "point." In a narrow sense of the word, all humor has a point. That is, all humor except for shaggy dog stories and other specific styles in which the laugh actually depends on the *absence* of a point.

> My wife says I make her sick. How did I know arsenic doesn't agree with her?

The "point" of this kind of stand-up comedy, of course, is misunderstanding of the idiomatic meaning of "make her sick." As it stands, it doesn't have much illustrative value.

But see how a Maine politician used the same basic funny idea to illustrate a very serious one.

> I understand some congressmen are saying that the fuel shortage is a good thing because it will help cool off the economy.
>
> Reminds me of the woman who was interviewed in the hospital after her husband had confessed to police he had been putting traces of arsenic in her jar of instant coffee.
>
> The reporters asked, "How do you feel about your husband now?"
>
> "Oh," she said, "he makes me sick."

It's still basically a double-meaning gag, but it now illustrates drastic understatement and makes a biting comment on a serious issue.

How to Pinpoint the Point

In Chapter 5 we saw how successful joke switchers break down the original joke into extremely simple and basic terms before they attempt to rebuild it. The same process works when speakers try to convert serious ideas into funny ideas.

When a serious idea is reduced to its simplest, most basic principles, the possibilities of finding humorous illustration are greatly broadened. The speaker has more room to work, and the range of targets, topics, and areas from which to construct funny ideas that dramatize and clarify the same basic point is widened.

Experienced speakers work something like this.

Serious idea to be humorized

The lack of harmony in our marketing department is not the fault of any one person or any one group of people. Each one has merit. We simply have too many different personality types all trying to work together on common objectives.

The basic, fundamental point

Each of the component parts is valid, but they don't fit together very well.

The basic funny idea

It's like having a number of different jig-saw puzzles all scrambled in the same box.

The final illustrative joke

The lack of harmony in our marketing department isn't the fault of any one person or group.

It's like a friend of mine who is a jigsaw puzzle fiend. One day his kids were playing with his puzzles and they put his Marilyn Monroe puzzle back in the same box with his Revolutionary War puzzle.

I asked him how he made out with things all mixed up.

"Oh," he said, "I did all right. But I never realized that George Washington had such sexy legs."

Once the speaker reduces the serious point to a simple, basic idea or principle, he can put any and all humor formulas and techniques to work to produce relevant and illustrative basic funny ideas. Once he has a promising assortment of basic funny ideas, he can easily multiply them into an even larger assortment of illustrative gags and jokes.

We've been discussing the process from the point of view of the *original* humorist. The same procedure works for the speaker who wants to *borrow* his illustrative humor. With a little editing, one of Henny Youngman's favorite gags serves as an excellent humorous interpretation of the basic point we've been working with.

The lack of harmony in our marketing department isn't the fault of any one person . . . or group. The people just aren't well matched.

Like the furrier who crossed a mink with a gorilla. He got a beautiful coat . . . but the sleeves are too long.

Whether a speaker uses original or borrowed humor, the job

of finding humorous illustrations for serious ideas is a matter of switching. Instead of switching a joke into a joke, the humorist switches a serious idea into a joke. The procedures are virtually identical.

How Humor Can Make a Point More Memorable

When an idea is illustrated humorously the audience is more likely to remember it. This is somewhat of a paradox because humor itself is difficult to remember. Humor is based on divergent and unusual associations and consequences. Psychologists can pretty well prove that unusual associations and consequences are harder to remember than usual ones. But when a speaker makes a point with humor, the audience pays more attention to the serious point, even if they can't remember the details of the humorous illustration. Experienced speakers who recognize the memory value of humor make doubly sure this happens by forging strong links between their serious ideas and their humorous versions.

Remember the old preacher's philosophy of making a speech? The modern platform humorist has revised it.

1. First I tell 'em what I'm going to tell 'em . . . seriously.

2. Then I tell 'em . . . humorously.

3. Then I tell 'em what I told 'em . . . seriously.

Here's a good example of the technique in action from the ready wit of a southern Illinois sales manager.

> When the economy slows down . . . that's the time to bring back some of the time tested promotions. When sales fall off you gotta promote . . . every good businessman knows that.
>
> Why, even the panhandlers on skid row are giving 30 days credit.
>
> There's a call girl in Springfield who has doubled her business just by putting in a lay-away plan.
>
> No matter what kind of business you're in . . . when business slows down . . . promote!

Whether his audience could repeat the two gags or not is not important. They walked out of the meeting with the idea "promote" etched indelibly in their minds.

How Humor Can Clarify a Point

Frequently a speaker will try to get across a serious idea that isn't easy for everyone to grasp. It may be too subtle for broad comprehension, or it may be too intricate and dull to command sufficient attention. Either way, humor can help clarify it.

The following joke came from an executive of a large discount chain, while he was talking at a trade association meeting.

> I overheard one of the younger men in our business complaining about overstocked warehouses ... too much inventory.
>
> It reminded me of a friend of mine who tried to explain to me why he didn't invest in the stockmarket.
>
> He said, "It's too unstable."
>
> I said, "What do you mean ... unstable?"
>
> He said, "Hell, the prices of the stocks keep going up and down."
>
> Please explain to me how anybody could make money in the stockmarket if the prices didn't go up and down.
>
> And, while you're at it, please explain to me how anybody could make money in mass merchandising if they didn't have masses of merchandise to sell.

Humorous clarification demands a strong link between the serious idea and the funny idea. If the funny idea doesn't clarify the serious point, it will do the opposite. It will produce further doubt or confusion.

Often a little editing can strengthen the link.

> Someone asked how I liked being the head of a department with only one employee. It's a little bit like the prostitute who had only one customer ... her husband.

A speaker friend of mine got a good laugh out of that, but it left the audience in some understandable confusion as to precisely what he meant. Recognizing this, he added a clarifying line the next time he used the gag. He not only achieved the clarification, he got a second laugh.

> She never achieved any real professional status.

Pleased with the result, he added a third laugh.

> She never made any money, either.

Humor not only can clarify difficult or obscure ideas, it can do so without patronizing or talking down to the audience, which is the danger of serious efforts to explain or amplify an idea. Genuinely humorous clarification does not insult an audience's intelligence.

How Humor Can Make a Point More Persuasive

Here we enter somewhat more controversial territory. Few will seriously challenge the claim that humor can add memorability and clarity to ideas if used intelligently for that purpose. But can humor actually persuade people? Can it actually change their minds, especially on issues that are emotionally strong and vital to their welfare? There are many who argue it can't. They argue that humor is great for *fortifying* beliefs, but not for *changing* them.

Persuasion isn't always a question of changing peoples' minds. Often it's more a matter of swaying someone from a tentative position that is weakly held, toward a strong conviction. Sometimes it's a matter of making a somewhat questionable idea seem more plausible.

> Mr. Dewey has come out fearlessly in favor of *Alice in Wonderland,* mother, and the home.

That quip by Harold Ickes, somewhat tame by today's standards, is credited with swaying a lot of votes for Harry Truman in the 1948 presidential race. It's highly unlikely that it persuaded any staunch Dewey supporters or many of his lukewarm backers, but it reputedly cut a wide swath through the fence straddlers, dramatizing the GOP candidate's alleged failure to deal with the relevant issues of the campaign.

Seymour Kleinman believes humor can be persuasive because of its ability to relieve tensions in difficult negotiations. As a top lawyer, he should know. Frequently, he says, a well-timed story can be the "clincher." Once, after receiving what he deemed to be an acceptable settlement offer in a difficult controversy, he was chagrined to hear his client ask for a day to think about it. When they returned the following day the opening gambit of the opposition lawyer was to withdraw the offer made the day before. The effect was traumatic to Mr. Kleinman and his client, who were certain that the next offer, if there was to be one, would be less favorable. To break the tension, the Manhatten attorney told this story:

> A guest in a prominent hotel called Room Service for breakfast and ordered warm orange juice, with pits and with pulp, two eggs sunnyside up but very lightly done and gooey, burned toast, and cold coffee in a dirty cup with lipstick smudges on the rim.
>
> The astonished bellboy said, "Sir, we can't make such a breakfast!"
>
> To which the guest replied, "Why not? You did yesterday."

The point was effectively made, and yesterday's offer was revived and the matter settled. Humor had its day and the opposition was virtually laughed into agreement.

Humor can also make contributions to another strong persuasive tool known to all experienced lawyers, diplomats, and other forensic experts.

Reductio ad absurdum is defined as the refutation of a proposition by demonstrating the inevitably absurd conclusion to which it could logically lead. If you'll think back to Chapter 9, in our discussion of advanced humor techniques we talked about humor built on ridiculous consequences, so reductio ad absurdum, in addition to being a classic argumentive tool, is also a Latin label for one of the strongest humor techniques.

Persuasion is one of civilization's most sophisticated art forms. Or, is it a science? Whichever it is, it is one of the great challenges in law, politics, advertising, and many other fields. We're not claiming that persuasion can always be helped by humor, anymore than we are claiming that all humor is persuasive. But the evidence is clear. When it comes at the right time and makes the right point humor can be a powerful persuasive tool.

The Advantages of a Humorous Title

Perhaps the most overlooked but most advantageous place to make a point humorously in a speech is in the title. Certainly the title ought to make a point, that is, a point beyond mere communication of the general subject. I'm sure we can agree that far too many speeches carry dull titles like these.

Some Observations About Productivity.

New Sources Of Revenue For Banks

It's pretty obvious that speech titles like those could be made far more interesting without resorting to humor.

Is Productivity Always Productive?

Hidden Profits In Banking—Some Of
Them Haven't Been Discovered Yet.

But some of the best public speakers like to make their speech titles both interesting and amusing, whenever the topic and occasion are appropriate. We saw a good example of this in Chapter 6.

Everything You've Always Wanted To Know
About Charitable Tax Deductions, But
Were Too Cheap To Ask.

Title humor follows most of the same rules and same formulas of any other kind of humor. This one was an alteration, a *complex* alteration, it's true, but an alteration, nonetheless.

Here's another.

Advertising Research, or, What You Do Know Can Hurt You.

Even puns can produce sharply pointed and amusing speech titles.

Maybe We Should Call Our Industry . . . Public Futilities.

Most successful humorous speech titles fall into the light, witty, epigrammatic category. Unlike gags, which are delivered audibly in a speech, titles are printed in programs and, thus, must endure inspection and reinspection by many people over a long period of time. They must withstand investigation and criticism by people who may not have heard the speech. So it's better to be more clever than funny, to be content with smiles rather than laughs. But, of all the places in a speech to make a point humorously, the title may be the best place of all because of its ability to attract interest in the speech and set the tone of the talk.

15

The Secret of Special Material . . . Keeping a Humor Notebook

While much of the successful humor heard from the speaker's platform is general and even universal in its appeal, most of the really accomplished rostrum wits take pride in "slanting" their humor toward the vocations, hobbies, subjects, and events in which a particular audience has a special interest.

The "show biz" comic calls anything that was written especially for him special material, no matter how general its slant. We're using the term to mean humor that is tailored for a specific audience.

It doesn't necessarily have to be intellectual or sophisticated humor.

> Some say that, for a physician, John has an over-developed interest in money. That he thinks about money more than medicine. I can't agree with that. But I must admit he's the only doctor I know who has both his MD and his CPA.

There's nothing especially brainy about that. Any reasonably educated adult can understand it. But it is nicely slanted toward the medical field.

We're not implying here that humor must be slanted to be funny. Doctors laugh at baseball jokes or go-go-girl jokes as well as at medical gags. But a specialized audience of any kind does seem to have a special appreciation for humor whose subject matter is slanted their way. This poses a special problem for the speaker. Slanted humor isn't easy to come by, especially that dealing with the subjects of most interest to business and professional men. You can't steal it from TV and nightclub comics because they can't afford to use anything that narrow in its appeal. Some of the trade and professional magazines contain a few choice items from time to time, but most don't. Most joke books and humor encyclopedias are notoriously short of it, and, what there is of it in these volumes is usually "slanted" only in the most superficial sense of the word, like this so-called "salesman" joke.

> Two salesmen were talking about the stock market. One said, "Are you a bull or a bear?" The other said, "I'm mainly a chicken."

That's just a "broker" or "investor" joke masquerading as a "salesman" joke. The subject is the stock market or the financial world, and switching the cast to salesmen, doctors, used car dealers, or atomic physicists doesn't change the subject—doesn't make it genuine special material.

The most reliable source for specially slanted material is the speaker's own head. He develops it himself either by skillfully editing and switching the subject matter of borrowed humor, or by building it from scratch. Either method requires original funny thinking, plus plenty of relevant and factual data about the subject in question.

Many speakers solve the problem by keeping a humor notebook, a classified listing of all the basic funny ideas, humor clues, tips and thought starters they think about or hear about on the subjects they usually speak about.

What Should Be Noted in a Humor Notebook?

A humor notebook is no different in principle from an artist's sketchbook. It contains all those valuable but fleeting ideas, notions, hunches, thoughts, and half-thoughts that often occur but are seldom remembered. That's the main value of keeping a humor notebook. It's a systematic way to remember anything and everything that might contribute to a humorous idea on a special subject. Just as an artist frequently sketches only portions of a scene or parts of a face, a humorist finds that even small remnants and particles of potentially funny ideas can grow into successful gags and quips after he's had the chance to mull them over in his mind. But neither the artist nor the humorist can mull over something he can't remember. So the answer is to make a humorous note of it.

Here's a neat little alteration that lay dormant in one speaker's notebook for months.

A pigment of his imagination.

The night before he was to address a New England group on the subject of public financing of the arts he turned it into a literate laugh.

> When an artist uses up more than ten square feet of canvas for just two or three little dabs of paint . . . I can only assume he is quite reluctant to give us any more than a small pigment of his imagination.

A New Jersey attorney put these two ideas down in the "Legal" section of his humor notebook.

Change of venue . . . change of underwear

No lo contendere . . . no lo comprendo

Out of those two quick notations came these four successful "legal" jokes.

> Change of venue? Hell, that judge wouldn't give you a change of underwear.

> A young law student asked a veteran criminal lawyer how he decides to ask for a change of venue. "Well," he said, "venue is like underwear. You know you need a change when you detect an unfavorable odor."

> My client was Puerto Rican, and, after discussing the case with him through an interpreter, we decided to plead no lo comprendo.

> The law can be very confusing even for a lawyer. Whenever I can't figure out what the judge is talking about, I usually plead no lo comprendo.

Those jokes are specifically and totally slanted toward an

audience that has both an interest and a knowledge of law, attorneys, judges, police officers, newsmen, and so on. Because of their inside slant, these lines are thoroughly enjoyable to such audiences.

The following pages contain entries from the humor notebooks of several talented speakers. They deal, of course, only with the subjects in which these speakers and their audiences are most interested. But the approach would be the same for any subject from architecture to zoology. Browse through these notes. Notice how the entries range from mere fragments to finished quips and gags. The least you'll get out of it will be further insight into the way funny thinkers think. And, hopefully, you will be inspired to start your own humor notebook on your own pet topics.

Pages from a Humor Notebook

Medicine

Transplants . . . of unlikely organs: appendix, head, warts, belly button, and so on.

Transplants . . . across social, sexual, political, ethnic or racial boundaries . . . the consequences.

Doctor puts Chinese stomach into Mexican . . . he's doing fine but he keeps asking for refried bean sprouts.

Transplanted Englishman's liver into Irishman . . . now he can't hold his liquor.

Doctor doesn't do transplants on foreigners . . . can't get parts.

Plastic surgery . . .

Funny combinations . . . Chinese plastic surgeon . . . did a beautiful job on my face . . . but my eyes slant.

Guy got a job in a plastics factory . . . as a surgeon.

Remove, removal . . . real vs. abstract . . .

The surgeon removed her ovaries . . . and her inhibitions.

He removed my appendix . . . and my money.

Surgeon removes a guy's hand . . . from his brother's pocket.

Trash removal, paint removers, and so on.

Take out . . . good double meanings . . .

The Dr. took out my appendix . . . then I took out his nurse.

Take my gall bladder . . . out.

Oriental surgery . . . Chinese take out.

Double take . . . removal of tonsils and adenoids.

Examinations, tests . . .

Doctors tested my elbow . . . found out I was a lush, alcoholic, and so on.

Doctors gave her a thorough examination . . . found out she was single, a nymphomaniac, promiscuous, a tramp . . . and so on.

They discovered my income was high . . . they discovered I had a lot of nerve.

Temperature, thermometer . . .

They put the thermometer in my mouth . . . found out I was a hot head.

My temperature was like my I.Q. . . . 98, below normal, above normal, and so on.

My temperature was normal for this time of year . . . but my brain was cloudy.

Take off your clothes, embarrassing, sensitive . . .

I'm always suspicious when a psychiatrist begins his examination by asking me to take off my clothes.

Doctor hostilities and aggressions . . .

Medicare . . . rival medical theories and practices . . . orthopedists vs. neurosurgeons . . . MDs vs. chiropractors . . . mal-practice suits and insurance costs . . . low incomes for interns . . . arrogance of older, "teaching" physicians and surgeons . . .

Substitute rival medical types for targets in ethnic jokes.

Dope ring . . . six chiropractors sitting in a circle.

How do you break a foot doctor's finger? Hit him in the nose.

Redefinition . . . Nasal rhinitis: snot nose.

"Open your mouth and say . . . yah."

"Hummmmm" called most frightening word in English language by H. Allen Smith.

Doctor keeps saying "hummm" as he examines patient . . . hummm . . . hummm . . . hummm . . . as he checks heart, lungs, throat, and so on. Then when the patient asks him for his diagnosis, it goes like this: "Humm hum . . . hum. hummmm-hum . . . hum-hum-hum-hum . . . hummmmmmmm."

Young doctors . . .

Needs a wet nurse cause he's not dry behind the ears.

Still calls his lab assistant "nursie."

Puns . . .

Dr. who's a great kidder. He really needles you.

Stitch . . . in stitches, stitch in time, sewing machine, seamstress, tailor, sewing circle.

X-Ray . . . sounds like X-Rated.

I.V. like "Ivy" . . . I.V. League.

Baseball

Destroy cliches of sports writers, announcers, and players:
"This game isn't over yet." "Game's never over 'til last man is out."

"He's got great desire." Yeah, but what good is desire when you're impotent?

Change-up? Can't even change his underwear.

Sucker pitch. He was a sucker to throw it.

Strike . . . requires organized labor . . . of pitcher and catcher.

That ump couldn't call a strike if he had the entire AFL-CIO behind him.

Mitt . . . German for "with"

> Player who drops mitt is "unmitigated." Similarily ... catcher who works without mitt and is named Gall ... is "Unmitigated Gall."

Foul tip ... bad advice

Foul line ... bad joke

Swing ...

> She was a third strike and he was a real swinger.
>
> He wanted to be a swinger, but his wife put the take sign on.
>
> A swing and a miss ... or Ms ... or Mrs.
>
> He didn't take a full swing ... more of a teeter-totter.

Batting odor ... Team stinks, just take a look at (or smell) the batting odor. Batting disorder ... they not only didn't know who's on first ... they didn't know who's up to bat.

Fair ball? Mediocre is a better word.

Shortstop ... He's short but he can't stop anything.

Receiver ...

> I've seen better receivers on handcranked telephones.
>
> Put down the receiver ... he deserves it.
>
> Team managed by a catcher is "in the hands of receiver."

Squeeze is on ... but the hit is off.

Hit and run vs. watch and walk.

Expansion ...

> It's an expansion team ... and they could use some expansion in their batting averages.
>
> For an expansion team they have too much contraction.
>
> They may be an expansion club ... but they haven't expanded enough yet to cover second base and left field.
>
> Expansion ... player's waistline.

Spring training ... not enough spring in it.

He can hit in the clutch . . . but not in the batters box.

He can chew gum and walk . . . but he can't chew tobacco and hit . . . mainly because he can't hit.

Ballpark figures . . . fat catcher, skinny pitcher, and so on.

Mounds Bar . . . where pitchers go after the game.

On deck . . . overboard . . . seasick . . . and so on.

It's hard to believe that a guy that bald ever came from the Bush Leagues.

"Back on the grass" . . . He's one outfielder who knows how to go back on the grass . . . unless the manager watches him pretty close.

He's got good hands . . . fast hands . . . just ask (girl). Also "good eye" . . . just ask his wife.

Last of the fifth . . . next time get a quart.

Line-up . . . I've seen better looking ones at police headquarters.

In the cellar . . . mouldy, mildewed . . . junk . . . trash . . . and so on.

Baseball . . . aptly named . . . appeals to base instincts.

Catcher in the Rye . . . pitcher full of martinis . . . manager loaded too.

National Pastime . . . past its time?

Hotels-Motels

So I went down to the front desk and talked to the madam . . . head masseuse . . . and so on.

Does this hotel have a massage parlor? This hotel *is* a massage parlor.

Every room has a mirror on the ceiling . . . presumably for people who want to comb their hair before they get out of bed.

They'll take any credit card. Leave your room unlocked and they'll take your luggage too . . . wallet . . . and so on.

Talk about courtesy . . . I know POW's who were treated better than that.

They don't have a 13th floor. They thought it would be bad luck. I got news . . . the 12th and the 14th floors are bad luck too.

There's no privacy . . . the walls are as thin as . . . well, instead of cleaning them with Mr. Clean . . . they have to use an eraser.

My room wasn't bugged . . . but the bed was.

Color TV . . . but black and white water.

Black and white TV . . . but the shower curtain is in living color.

No animals allowed . . . but you should have seen the pigs in the bar.

The swimming pool has beautiful blue water . . . but I lost interest when I found out how they did it. Ty-D-bol!

Elevators on the outside of the building . . . unfortunately, so are the bathrooms/toilets.

Hotel chain . . . and this was its weakest link.

Reservations . . . *serious* reservations.

Hotel so cheap . . . paper bathtowels . . . the penthouse was a house trailer parked on the roof . . . the airport courtesy bus was a dune buggy. In the men's room they had pay urinals. They rented you the room . . . then they offered to rent you furniture to go in it.

This hotel was so cheap . . . there's a $3.00 charge on your bill for "Flushing." And they don't mean a phone call to Long Island.

In San Francisco . . . a Chinese Hotel . . . not only was the bathroom at the end of the hall . . . you had to buy a ticket to take a shower. The sign said . . . no tickee, no washee.

I asked for a "double." They gave me a room with one twin bed but two chairs.

Uncomfortable beds . . .

> Like a waterbed . . . with no water.
>
> I won't say the beds are lousy . . . but the bellhops do a land-office business on the side . . . selling Doan's Pills.

Peace and quiet . . .

> I'm always suspicious when I ask for a nice quiet room and the desk clerk issues me a set of ear plugs.
>
> I worried about the noise from the bar in the lobby . . . the clerk said don't worry about that . . . it's the bowling alley on the roof that keeps 'em awake.
>
> I hung out a sign for the maids "Please do not disturb." The maids didn't disturb me . . . it was the guy in the next room practicing his zither all night.

Lazy staff . . . Bell Captain has "Please Do Not Disturb" sign on his desk.

Stupid staff . . .

> I told them my bed was too soft . . . that I needed a bed board. They brought me the board . . . but they took my mattress.
>
> I called room service and said I needed something for my stomach. They brought me a cummerbund.
>
> I asked room service to bring me a quart of something good. They did . . . homogenized milk.

Room Service . . . room needed lots of service: plumber, painter, interior decorator, and so on.

Room Service . . . had to dial long distance to get it . . . had an unlisted number . . . you have to go down in the lobby and take a number.

Salesmen

He sets his own goals . . . number one is to get to the bar by mid-afternoon.

He sets his own quotas . . . three martinis a day.

He knows how to keep his customers happy . . . now if he could just learn how to sell them.

He refuses to take "no" for an answer, but he sure gets a lot of "maybes."

Sales incentive . . . poverty . . . unemployment . . . bar bill . . . alimony.

Motivation . . . thumb screws . . . torture . . . wine, women, and stereo equipment.

Sales agent . . . I remember when a good salesman could sell himself. Now he needs an agent.

Sales representative . . . I thought a good salesman could represent himself.

He thinks hard sell means a tough customer.

His idea of soft sell . . . is to only grab one lapel . . . is to only put his toe in the door.

Self starter . . . unfortunately a self stopper too.

Order taker . . .

> My boss says he doesn't want me to be an order taker. So why does he keep giving me orders?
>
> The only orders he gets are from his boss.

Commission . . .

> Commission vs. omission.
>
> He's out of commission. Out of orders too.
>
> The best commission he ever got was in the Polish army.

He sold himself a bill of goods . . . then tried to collect a commission on it.

Territorial imperative . . . means this is your territory and it's imperative that it be covered twice a month.

How can they say sales are "soft" when they're so "hard."

Foot in door . . . foot in mouth.

> "No, no, Murphy . . . not your hand . . . your foot."

High pressure salesmanship . . .

> He could sell a side of beef to a vegetarian.
>
> He could sell a paint by numbers kit to the Guggenheim.
>
> He could sell surgical tools to a Christian Scientist.
>
> He could sell a yarmulke to a Moslem.
>
> He could sell a tuxedo to Tarzan.

He could sell a matzo ball to an Arab.

He could sell a pork chop to an orthodox Rabbi.

You gotta know the territory . . . you also gotta know the secretaries.

Fat salesman . . .

He isn't filling out many orders, but he's sure filling out his clothes.

Every sale he makes is gross.

Sure his gross is high . . . yours would be too if you ate like that.

His sales are up . . . so is his weight.

He covers a big territory . . . especially around the middle.

Sales pitch . . . wild . . . lots of curves . . . in the dirt . . .

He's got so much gall his customers call him Charles De.

Close a sale? He can't close his mouth.

Every salesman has to learn how to sell himself . . . and for (NAME) . . . that takes some real high pressure selling.

It's tough for him to sell himself . . . it's inferior merchandise.

I know one door-to-door salesman who makes so few house calls his boss calls him "Doc."

16

What to Do When
Your Humor Isn't Funny

What can a speaker do when after he follows all the principles and techniques for good humor the laughs still don't come? That is, the laughs don't come *most* of the time. Everybody loses laughs now and then, even the top professionals. But what can you do if you find you still can't make even *some* of the people laugh *some* of the time? I hope that Chapters 1 through 15 of this book have made the subject of humor a little less elusive for you. But it's still elusive. It's still a very delicate blend of respect and irreverence, honesty and deception, logic and illogic, sense and nonsense, and discretion and indiscretion.

What can a speaker do if after conscientiously studying humor psychology, construction, editing, switching, and formula following, he still finds it nearly impossible to stimulate that remarkable, involuntary response known as laughter?

Can Humor Defects Be Diagnosed?

Can an unsuccessful humorist learn to analyze his failures and correct them? Can he find out what's wrong and avoid making the same mistakes over and over again? He can if he's willing to become a dedicated student of the art of making people laugh—a real humor hobbyist.

Many outstanding platform laugh-getters owe at least part of their "talent" to the fact that they are as intrigued by humor failure as they are pleased with humor successes. To them, a "bomb" is a valuable feedback, and part of continual trial-and-error experimentation.

What is this trial-and-error research, and how is it conducted? Some speakers conduct it on the speakers platform. They watch and listen carefully for audience reaction to each gag or story. From speech to speech they tinker with their material and make adjustments to keep boosting its laugh power.

Other renowned laugh-getters, like General Motors executive Gail Smith, like to pre-test gags and jokes among individuals and small groups *before* they use them in a real speech. Just as dedicated golfers hit buckets of balls at a driving range, these dedicated humor students hit buckets of gags during the many informal practice sessions available to them everyday—at lunch, in the bar, playing golf, tennis, or cards—anywhere and everywhere they can find individuals and small gatherings of people whose backgrounds, personalities, and positions make them likely to react to humor much like the audiences they usually address. While it's true that individuals and small groups seldom respond exactly like a large audience, neither does a golf driving range offer all the mental and physical hazards of a championship course. But that's a poor excuse for not practicing to better your score.

The Most Frequent Humor Problems

Admittedly there are dozens of things that can go wrong with humor, including the weather. But any systematic trial-and-error humor research must begin with some likely areas for probing and testing. After listening carefully and analytically to hundreds and hundreds of performances by both successful and unsuccessful laugh-seeking speakers I am convinced that laugh failure most often stems from one of these three common defects.

1. Inept delivery
2. Weak targets
3. Weak ammunition

If this list sounds too simple in view of the great complexities of humor psychology, remember that we're addressing ourselves *only* to the problem of *not* getting a laugh. A humorist can have lots of other problems and still get laughs. He can be corny and still get laughs. He can be offensive and still get laughs. He can be unfair and still get laughs. He can be insufferably egotistical and still get laughs. He can be all of these things and still get laughs. But when he repeatedly gets *no* laughs, the cause is most apt to lie in the ineptitude of the delivery, the low vulnerability of the target, or the small caliber of the ammunition.

Testing Joke Delivery

For many people, joke telling is the hardest part of making people laugh. Fortunately it's also the easiest phase of humor to tinker with, the easiest thing to test and retest until you begin to get the feel of what works and what doesn't.

There's nothing to prevent a speaker from telling the same joke 40 times to 40 different people, varying his delivery each time and making astute observations of the results. But it should be the *same* joke. Nothing can wreck research quicker than too many variables. If the humor experimenter keeps changing his delivery technique, but also keeps changing other ingredients, target and ammunition, for example, he cannot be sure that the changes in response were caused mainly by changes in delivery.

What specific aspects of delivery should he be tampering with? That is, what aspects of delivery are most apt to be causing trouble and also are most susceptible to experimentation? Among speakers who consistently get few laughs, *emphasis* is the most common delivery defect. Emphasis problems are of several different types.

1. Failure to stress the key words, especially the "revelation."
2. Stressing non-essential words, which has the effect of reducing the emphasis on the key words.
3. Failure to pause after critically important ideas. This is sometimes looked on as a matter of "timing," but it is more accurately a question of emphasis and audience comprehension.

Admittedly, this book is written for people who already have a knack for bringing proper emphasis to serious ideas. But that experience and talent, although extremely helpful, does not always lead automatically to effective emphasis of humorous ideas.

If your own public speaking skills and the early chapters of this book have not led you to a sensitive feel for effective humorous emphasis, now's the time to get in some serious and objective practice. Nothing can make or break a good joke like effective or ineffective emphasis.

> He can't hold his liquor. But he sure can hold other people's liquor.

A gag like that presents the simplest possible problem in humorous emphasis.

> He can't hold his liquor. But he sure can hold *other* people's liquor.

That's about all there is to it. Yet, some speakers will find any number of ways to mess it up, even to the point of stressing "his" in the setup, thereby running a serious risk of giving the gag away prematurely.

This one's a little tougher.

> The girl says, "I'm telling you for the last time. Take your hand off my knee." The guy says, "I knew you'd give in."

It should be obvious that "last time" is a critically important idea in that gag. It makes the vital connection with "give in." But there are other words that need attention too if the audience is to feel the full impact of the joke. How does a speaker handle all this emphasis without de-emphasizing something important?

> The girl says, "I'm *telling* you for the *last time* (BEAT) Take your *hand* off my *knee.*" The guy says, "I *knew* you'd *give in.*"

Here, the speaker has managed to emphasize several ideas, but has maintained the strongest emphasis on "last time" by using not one, but two, emphasis techniques. He's given it the loudest voice and he's followed it with a short pause, or "beat" as the professionals say. This extra emphasis on the critically important "last time" permits him to give meaningful secondary emphasis to other words and ideas that are important to the emotional impact of the joke.

Some jokes contain so many vital ideas leading to the payoff that mere word stress won't handle the job. The speaker *must* use pauses to prevent chaos, to allow the audience to process all the strategic information step by step.

> The fact is, Joe has always been fat. When he was an infant, instead of a baby carriage, his parents had to use a forklift.

There's a lot of visual imagery in that gag, imagery that must be transmitted clearly to the audience if the punchline is going to have enough punch. Strategic pauses or beats help transmit the picture.

> The fact is, Joe has *always* been *fat.* (BEAT) When he was an *infant,* (BEAT) instead of a *baby carriage,* (BEAT) his parents had to use a *forklift.*

If all this sounds obvious and elementary, congratulations! Emphasis is probably not one of your problems. But if it sounds vague or appears to be unnecessary hair-splitting, you may be in for some real surprises when you test radically different ways of emphasizing some of your joke failures. Never discount the importance of emphasis in joke telling. Unless you're pretty sure you have a real knack for it, you'd better do some serious trial-and-error experimentation.

Another common defect in joke delivery involves what may best be called *authority.* This problem is more difficult to explain and correct than emphasis. It has to do with attitude, and attitude borders on acting. It's probably the closest a successful humorist needs to get to theatrical skills.

They say that "acting is believing," and believability is one of the dimensions we're talking about when we say a joke must be delivered with some authority. We're not talking about the kind of authority involved in being boss. We're using the word authority to mean "knowledgeability" and "reliability."

> Joe is a man who stands ten feet tall. That is, providing he's up on a four-and-a-half foot platform.

The success of a put-down like this depends greatly on the authority with which the speaker delivers the opening setup line. It must carry the implication that we are, indeed, going to hear some nice things about Joe's courage and his convictions.

Attitude is separate from emphasis. There are dozens of different ways to emphasize this setup. Here, perhaps, are the most logical.

Joe is a man who stands *ten feet tall.*

Joe is a man who stands ten feet *tall.*

Joe *is* a man who stands ten feet tall.

Joe is a man who stands ten feet tall.

Joe is a man . . . who stands *ten feet* tall.

Joe is a man who stands . . . ten feet tall.

But none of those emphasis patterns guarantees effective attitude. All six versions can be delivered with an effective or ineffective attitude.

The authority and believability factor in joke telling can be damaged or destroyed very subtly. Because he doesn't personally find the joke terribly amusing, the speaker may subconsciously give it short shrift. Remember, it isn't what *you* think is funny that counts. It's what the *audience* thinks is funny. Because it's only a joke, the speaker may just joke his way through it. Again, this is very unprofessional. Nothing's more serious than getting laughs. The speaker may have the opposite problem. He may be so uptight and overly concerned about the laugh that he takes the job too seriously. It's primarily a question of, as the football coaches and sales managers say, proper mental attitude. Proper mental attitude *is* as important in humor as in any other field.

Although attitude is not as tangible as emphasis, it can be tinkered with and tested nonetheless. So, if the ideas in Chapter 1 haven't improved your joke delivery to the point where you can get a laugh, now's the time to begin some intelligent trial-and-error experimentation.

1. Pick out some short, simple, but solid jokes—jokes you feel confident are well-targeted and well-loaded for your kind of audience.

   These should be gags you know will be funny if delivered effectively. Maybe you borrowed them from other speakers who have used them with success. Maybe they come from a good joke book. Whatever the source, they should be reasonably simple gags that have been tested and proved to be funny to the kinds of people you usually give your speeches to.

2. Memorize them **exactly as** they were worded when they were performed successfully. Don't change words or word order. If one or more of these gags just doesn't seem to be written in your "style" get some more you can feel comfotrable with. Don't let "style" be a cop-out for inept delivery technique, however. Any effective public speaker should be able to deliver a simple gag effectively no matter what "style" he thinks he has.

3. Study them as intently, as carefully, and as slyly as a lawyer would study a paragraph in a contract if he were looking for a loophole.

Don't take anything for granted. Ask yourself why this word was used, why this sentence seems to have been worded backwards, and so on.

Plug in everything you've learned about humor psychology and construction. Remember that when you study these simple gags you're really studying "verbal magic tricks." Apply the principles of emphasis and attitude we've just discussed.

4. Try to formulate some promising alternative ways to deliver the gags, remembering that what you think may be the most effective way to deliver them may actually be the least effective. In other words, operate in the spirit of true research, prepare some clearly different test approaches.

If you like, have some associates who can deliver jokes effectively throw in some suggestions, or you might even have them deliver the gags their way into a tape recorder so you can mimic them.

5. Start a systematic program of selecting individuals and small groups, and testing these alternative delivery approaches. Begin with what you think would be the most logical, then correct for windage if the laughs don't come. Keep notes in your head or on paper as to what works and your conclusions as to why it works.

Remember you're not merely trying to learn how to tell *these* jokes well, but how to tell *any* joke well.

6. Don't stop after a few trials, even if the results are very favorable. Keep testing until you develop great confidence in the results.

Humorous Target Practice

Not nearly as complicated, but just as valuable, is the testing of humorous targets. When an audience laughs at a joke it laughs at *someone*. When it doesn't laugh, the trouble may be that the speaker tried to get it to laugh at someone it didn't particularly want to laugh at. That's what we mean by a weak target, someone for whom the audience doesn't have any special negative feelings or minor hostilities, no competitive rivalries.

> I'll tell you, Peter has a mouth like a New York massage parlor. Open 24 hours a day.

The success of a gag like that depends almost entirely on the target, on the reputation of Peter's mouth. Many speakers make the mistake of choosing targets almost solely on the basis of the target's *familiarity* to the audience. But target familiarity is not nearly as important as target *vulnerability*. While it's true that people enjoy laughing at familiar, local targets more than at unfamiliar, distant ones, they *most* enjoy laughing at targets that are *vulnerable*. They enjoy laughing at the controversials: loud mouths, big shots, dumb-dumbs, the local playboy, or the local sex symbol.

Advertising agency president Jerry Birn knows how to pick good targets. This gag was the biggest laugh-getter out of a dozen good ones he used at a large company meeting. The audience included clerks and secretaries, as well as executives of all sizes, shapes, and salaries.

> We'd like to bring _____ up here to the podium to say a few words to you. But, as you know, _____ is really tall. So tall . . . we'd have to raise the microphone. And you know how the management feels about raising anything.

It was a blockbuster, not just because of the wit, primarily because the target was "management." As Jerry points out, "You can almost always get a laugh at a company party by picking on management."

When a speaker is familiar with his audience he should know how to choose vulnerable targets with relative ease. He should know who the fall guys and fall girls are. He should know where the bodies are buried, in whose closets the dirty linen is hung. He should know who does what to whom, both officially and unofficially. He should know about the frictions and conflicts, the boos, and the boo-boos.

What should a speaker do if he's not sufficiently familiar with his audience to single out the best butts for his jokes? Some speakers make a science of researching an unfamiliar audience in advance. They'll discuss possible targets, openly or slyly, with key members of the organization. If such advance sleuthing is impractical, they'll go with general targets, on judgment. They'll attack management, competitors, and the various occupational, political, national, ethnic, or even racial individuals and groups that their particular audience is most likely to want to laugh at.

As logical and simple as these fundamentals are, the beginner who keeps striking out while trying to bat out laughs may simply be doing a bad job of picking his targets. So he should experiment vigorously to become more "target conscious" and to improve his target selection.

Many gags are ideal for target practice.

_____ is so oversexed . . . whenever he hears the term "foreign affairs" he thinks they're talking about some guy who has an ethnic mistress.

Gags like that and millions more can be used for almost unlimited target switching to give the would-be laugh-getter a more acute sense of target vulnerability.

Target practice, then, consists of this simple regimen.

1. Take some good strong gags that have strong surprising insults in them, but are general enough that they could be told about a broad range of people, including you.
2. Tell them to a series of individuals and small groups, changing the target in an effort to keep boosting the laugh power. But don't change anything else.
3. Study the results. Try to understand why Ed's goof is funnier than Joe's, why your embarrassment is funnier than someone else's, why an executive's weight problem is funnier than his secretary's. In other words, try to become more "target conscious."

Testing Humorous Ammunition

Often when a speaker fails to get a laugh it's because he didn't fire a big enough bullet. His target may have been vulnerable, but his ammunition was weak. Every speaker makes this mistake occasionally, but some do it consistently. They don't seem to realize the importance of aggression in the laugh process. The result is humor that goes "pop" instead of "bang," jokes that fizzle instead of exploding.

Many social scientists believe laughter is actually a highly refined, civilized descendant of jungle aggression—a socially acceptable act of violence. And many successful funnymen and funnywomen keep experimenting, consciously or subconsciously, to find the levels of humorous aggression that will produce the most violent laughter. This probing and testing usually leads them to have most confidence in the so-called "gut ammunition" we discussed earlier in the book. Gut ammunition is related to the most repressed ideas and the most objectionable human defects—to sex, elimination, obesity, dishonesty, greed, vanity, laziness, and stupidity, to mention most of the biggies.

Even these big bullets come in different sizes. Here are four different "quack doctor" jokes. Each contains some gut ammunition. For example, all four suggest that the physician is either totally untrained, stupid, or crazy. But, notice how, even above that threshold, the caliber of the ammunition increases considerably from gag to gag.

> Talk about a quack doctor! I knew something was wrong when he put his stethoscope in my mouth and began to listen to my tonsils.

> Talk about a quack doctor! I knew something was wrong when he put his foot on my chest and tried to shove his stethoscope up my nose.

> Talk about a quack doctor! I knew something was wrong when he began to listen to my chest . . . with his proctoscope.

> Talk about a quack doctor! I knew something was wrong when he began to examine my throat with his proctoscope.

The ammunition in the first version confines itself to stupidity. The second introduces the element of uncomfortable violence. The third has no violence, but it brings in the powerful image of the traditional instrument for bowel examination and thus adds scatology to the thrust of the gag. The fourth has not one, but two elements of scatology, the imagery of the proctoscope plus confusion of the two major orifices of the body.

Among males, these four gags usually test like this for laugh power.

1. Amusing
2. Funny
3. Funnier
4. Funniest

Here are three more with decidedly ascending levels of aggression.

> I'm willing to give my life to this business . . . but not my weekends.

> I'm willing to give my heart and soul to this business . . . but not my kidneys.

> I'm willing to neglect my wife and kids for this business . . . but not my mistress.

Again, the relative laugh power of the gags is closely related to the degree to which they assault repressed ideas and attack revered social institutions. But ammunition doesn't have to deal with sex, elimination, adultery, and other repressed or anti-social subjects to be high caliber.

> Short? He is so short he thinks Sammy Davis Jr. is a basketball star.

> Eddie has everything it takes to be a sports super star. Big heart . . . big hands . . . big mouth.

Nor does a speaker have to avoid intellectual words and ideas in order to fire powerful ammunition.

> Henry is so lazy . . . he thinks that George is hyperactive.

If George is widely known for a shortage of nervous energy and the audience fully understands the term "hyperactive," it becomes a big caliber intellectual bullet.

Make no mistake about it, humorous ammunition can be too high in caliber. Some speakers have that problem, like the guy who goes duck hunting with a machine gun. But when a speaker consistently has a problem getting any laugh at all, when he keeps drawing outbursts of silence with his jokes and stories, he may simply be trying to hunt bears with a sling shot. Actually, it's not very hard for a speaker to determine when his ammunition is too strong. People will usually tell you, if you ask. They may tell you even if you don't ask. But when your ammunition isn't strong enough, they just don't laugh. If you ask them why it wasn't funny they aren't likely to say "because the ammunition was too weak." Chances are they don't know what's wrong. They just don't think it's funny. Overly aggressive humor usually draws some kind of laugh. It may be an embarrassed laugh, even a laugh that's quickly followed by a protest. But total silence is an indication that it's not aggressive enough.

Whether or not you're using the right caliber ammunition is a researchable, testable proposition. Just start putting some bigger bullets in the gun and fire them on your humor practice range. Don't guess. Test. Why risk offending a large and important audience when you can offend individuals and small groups? And immediately apologize and explain your motives, if necessary.

Step by step, the testing procedure goes like this.

1. Study some of the jokes that have been failures for you and assess the strength of the aggressive ideas. Do most of them seem to be slaps on the wrist rather than jabs on the nose?

2. If so, look for some bigger bullets to fire at the same targets. Keep the research reliable, change only the ammunition.

   If you're working with borrowed gags, pick tougher ones. If you're creating your own or switching, try to add more aggression, more gut ammo.

3. Fire them at strategically selected audience samples, repeatedly, adjusting fire power as you go.

4. Study the results and try to draw some conclusions about the relationship between the strength of the ammunition and the strength of the laughs. Try to develop an understanding of why the boss's fat stomach is funnier than a secretary's thick ankles, why the local Lothario's losing efforts in the stenographic pool are funnier than his poor memory or his late arrival at work. Keep testing and studying the results until you develop the ability to choose the right bullet for your game consistently.

Can Humor Research Be Trusted?

Is humor research reliable? Can you have any confidence in the results?

Humor research isn't infallible, but neither is much of the opinion sampling on which million dollar marketing and advertising decisions are made. Any research that involves opinions and ideas runs the risk of being inaccurate because of the tendency people have to react to questions the way they think they are *supposed* to feel rather than the way they really *do* feel.

Fortunately, when it comes to humor, it isn't easy for most people to hide their true opinions. As the professional comics say, funny is funny. If they laugh, it's funny. You can count on it. Conversely, if they *don't* laugh, something's wrong, even if your "test audience" assures you that "it was really very amusing."

You can test your humor systematically and scientifically in a very informal fashion without your friends and associates ever realizing they are being used as guinea pigs, meaning they should have no motive to try to hide or force a laugh.

Once a speaker develops the habit and knack of researching his delivery and material he'll begin to raise his L.Q. (Laugh Quotient). He'll also develop a much greater understanding of humor. And he'll have become a student of one of the most satisfying and absorbing of all subjects.

Index